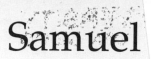

Samuel

Radical Puritan

Samuel Adams 1722–1803

NATIONAL UNIVERSITY
LIBRARY   SAN DIEGO

Samuel Adams

Radical Puritan

William M. Fowler, Jr.
Northeastern University

Edited by Oscar Handlin

 LONGMAN

An imprint of Addison Wesley Longman, Inc.

New York • Reading, Massachusetts • Menlo Park, California • Harlow, England
Don Mills, Ontario • Sydney • Mexico City • Madrid • Amsterdam

Acquisitions Editor: Bruce Borland
Developmental Editor: Lily P. Eng
Supervising Project Editor: Lois Lombardo
Project Coordination and Text Design: York Production Services
Cover Design: Kay Petronio
Manufacturing Manager: Hilda Koparanian
Electronic Page Makeup: York Production Services
Printer and Binder: R. R. Donnelley & Sons Company, Inc
Cover Printer: The Lehigh Press, Inc.

Library of Congress Cataloging-in-Publication Data

Fowler, Lillian M., 1944–
    Samuel Adams : radical puritan / William M. Fowler.
      p. cm.
    Includes bibliographical references (p.   ) and index.
    ISBN 0-673-99293-4
      1. Adams, Samuel, 1722–1803. 2. Politicians—United States—
Biography. 3. United States—History—Revolution, 1775–1783.
4. United States. Declaration of Independence—Signers—Biography.
5. Puritans—United States—Biography. I. Title.
E302.6.A2F69 1997
973.3'13'092—dc20   96-31033
[B]   CIP

Copyright © 1997 by Addison-Wesley Educational Publishers Inc.

All rights reserved. No part of this book may be used or reproduced, stored in retrieval system, or transmitted, in any form or by any means, electronic, mechanical, photocopying, recording, or otherwise, without the prior written permission of the publisher. Printed in the United States.

ISBN 0-673-99293-4
1234567890-DOC-99989796

LSR
"The World's Greatest Editor"

Contents

Editor's Preface		ix
Author's Preface		xi
CHAPTER 1	Puritan Beginnings	1
CHAPTER 2	Harvard and Home	15
CHAPTER 3	Rumblings	30
CHAPTER 4	The Battle Begins	43
CHAPTER 5	Sons of Liberty	57
CHAPTER 6	Townshend and Troops	72
CHAPTER 7	Boston Under Siege	85
CHAPTER 8	Massacre	100
CHAPTER 9	Tea and Intolerables	113
CHAPTER 10	The First Continental Congress	128
CHAPTER 11	Independence	145
CHAPTER 12	The New Republic	161
Bibliography		179
Index		183

Editor's Preface

Samuel Adams occupied a unique place among the founders of the American republic. He lived through all the events that led up to the ultimate separation from Britain, survived the war of independence, experienced the difficulties of establishing a constitutional federal republic, and served as governor of one of the more important states in the young nation. Yet unlike Washington, Jefferson, and Madison, he was not an aristocratic landowner by family, nor a soldier or lawyer by profession. Nor did he stem from a line of well-to-do merchants like the leaders from New York or Rhode Island.

Adams was an artisan as his father before him had been; men who worked for a living—not rich, not poor, middling— not country born but bred and reared in the city. His career in politics also reflected the interests and ideas of people like himself, independent craftsmen (carpenters, tailors, bakers, brewers) proud of their callings and of the sweat of their brows by which they earned a living. Quick to recognize their grievances, they promptly took to the streets in search of redress and coordinated their efforts in the town meeting, which in time supplied Samuel Adams an effective platform for leadership.

Gradually his perspective widened from the local to the continental scale. The horizons of his political views expanded from the town to the state and to the nation. All along Adams insisted on the central role of the *covenant*, of a voluntary agreement among participants who ruled themselves by consent. Just as in their relationship to God, men and women retained their liberty through accepting the divine will of their own accord, and so too in politics they remained free so long as they themselves created the government that ruled them.

William Fowler's lively book describes the long and eventful life of key figures in the development of the early republic. In doing so it also clarifies a significant aspect of American life.

Oscar Handlin

Author's Preface

In the pantheon of American heroes called the Founding Fathers, Samuel Adams holds a special place. He seems the most human. He lacked Jefferson's intellect and Washington's stature. He was as unworldly as Franklin was worldly. Adams had the common touch, and the people of Boston loved him for it. He was short, a bit paunchy, and ordinarily he dressed in clothes that looked as if they had been handed down by a more prosperous relative. Those who liked him referred to him as serious, virtuous, and patriotic. Others simply saw him as evil. But everyone agreed he could be a dangerous man.

My perspective on Adams derives from many years of teaching and writing about Boston and the American Revolution. I first became seriously interested in Adams while I was preparing a biography of John Hancock (*The Baron of Beacon Hill,* 1980). My work with Hancock brought me into close contact with Adams. It was an uneasy alliance between these two men. Hancock knew how to trim his sails and ride out the storms. Adams was a radical Puritan who hardly ever trimmed and despised those who did. Stern and unyielding Adams, "The Great Incendiary," led Boston into revolution.

What motivated Samuel Adams? My answer to this question informs my interpretation of Adams. Driven by his sense of covenant, he believed that the people of his community were bound to one another through a common history and reverence for virtue and simplicity. It was, he believed, his duty, and that of the men and women who shared his vision, to preserve this society. When the forces of king and Parliament threatened to destroy this world, Samuel Adams rebelled. In this sense Adams was a classic radical, a person who wished to return to the roots of his society. Once let loose, however, the momentum of revolution could not be easily contained. With sadness and irony, Samuel Adams watched as the Revolution released forces that celebrated and extolled the individual more than the corporate community. Adams detested much of what he saw in this new America. Instead of returning to the halcyon days of the "city upon a hill," Adams's world pushed forward into one of economic self-interest and rampant individualism.

In the aftermath of the Revolution, while others of his generation recognized and adapted to these changes, Adams railed against them. As a result he became an anachronism, an old and haunting figure in Boston, revered for what he had done, a quaint reminder of the past.

That past, however, is very much with us today. After more than two centuries the American republic is still struggling with the question of covenant. What is it that Americans owe to one another as citizens? What is it that Americans ought to expect from government and government from them? What is the role of virtue and morality in American society? It remains an ongoing debate.

Although only one person can use a keyboard at a time, no author does his or her job alone. As has long been the case I owe a considerable debt to Northeastern University. The librarians in the Snell Library have continued their long tradition of tolerance and graciousness as they deal with my innumerable requests. The provost was kind enough to help support me through his research fund. And although they may not realize it, my colleagues in the history department were critical to my work inasmuch in their conversation and questions they prompted me to ask questions that might otherwise have eluded me. A special thanks, of course, goes to Linda Smith Rhoads, my associate at *The New England Quarterly,* for her keen eye and good sense.

Boston is blessed with wonderful institutions supporting the work of scholars. My deepest thanks goes to all those who have helped me at the Massachusetts Historical Society, Boston Athenaeum, and the New England Historic Genealogical Society. The New York Public Library and the New York Historical Society were also generous in their assistance.

Finally, to my family Marilyn, Alison, and Nathaniel, I say thanks once more.

William M. Fowler, Jr.

Samuel Adams

Radical Puritan

CHAPTER 1

Puritan Beginnings

❖
❖

It was an elegant funeral, totally out of keeping with the simple wishes of the deceased. Boston, however, was determined to say good-bye to Samuel Adams in a manner it deemed befitting its hero.

On Thursday afternoon at four, the procession assembled at Adams's house on Winter Street just off the Common. His casket was carried out of his simple home and placed on a carriage. As the cortege moved eastward toward Washington Street, a large gathering of dignitaries fell in behind. Not since the funeral of Adams's fellow revolutionary, and sometime friend, John Hancock, who had been laid to rest almost exactly ten years before, had Boston witnessed such a spectacle.

Behind the casket followed Adams's wife Elizabeth and their only child Hannah with her husband Thomas Wells. First in order after the family appeared the "Marshall of the United States" accompanied by the "Legislative, Judicial, and Executive Officers of the United States." Some among the spectators smiled at the delicious irony. Solemn federal officials were dutifully paying their respects to a man who had long viewed the government of the "United States" with studied cynicism. Nonetheless, wise politicians all, they well understood that proximity to Adams, even in death, was still worth a few votes.

After the national bigwigs came a horde of local politicos: the sheriff of Suffolk County; members of the commonwealth's Executive Council, Senate, and House of Representatives; judges of the supreme judicial and superior courts; and the president and professors of Harvard College; selectmen of the town of Boston; overseers of the poor; members of the Board of Health; foreign consuls; members of the American Academy of Arts and Sciences; officers of the militia; and, finally, a large number of "Citizens and strangers." Clearly, the great "democrat's" funeral had a very hierarchical arrangement.

The long procession snaked its somber way north on Washington Street. As it treaded quietly through the streets, bells pealed from every church tower, and cannons fired at one-minute intervals. Shops along the route were closed. When the mourners reached the Old State House, scene of so many events in Adams's life, they wound around the building and up Court Street, onto Tremont, and through the gates of the Old Granary to the Adams family tomb. After listening to a few words of graveside committal, the crowd melted back into the streets of the town.

"Born in Boston, died in Boston" might have been a suitable epitaph for Samuel Adams. For more than half a century, he had been the most important and renowned political figure in a town famous for its politicians. Born on 16 September 1722, Adams was the fifth generation of the Adams family born in Massachusetts. The first Adams to land in Massachusetts was "Henry Adams of Braintree, the sixteenth generation from Ap Adams who came out of the Marches of Wales at a very remote period." Henry Adams brought with him eight sons and was himself the great-great-grandfather of both Samuel Adams and John Adams. It was John who in his own lifetime erected a granite column at his family's burial site to honor his ancestor so that future generations might know of their "piety, humility, simplicity, prudence, patience, temperance, frugality, industry, and perserverance" in the hope that they might imitate these virtues.

About 1684, when he was barely 23, Samuel's grandfather, John, married Hannah Webb. Their first child, a girl Hannah, died in infancy. Two years later another child, a son John, arrived.

Braintree was a pleasant and quiet community, but good land was becoming increasingly scarce and, in any case, John had shown little inclination to farm. So his departure could hardly have surprised the family.

With a population approaching seven thousand, Boston was a bustling, energetic place, its harbor tucked neatly behind the protective shield of its outlying islands. Exceeded only by London and Bristol, the town's registered fleet ranked third in the empire. In the half century since its founding, John Winthrop's "city upon a hill" had become a major port crowded with vessels from all parts of the Atlantic world and beyond.

In 1688 the town celebrated the news that the quasi-Catholic King James II had been deposed; in his place Parliament had offered the throne to William of Orange and his wife Mary, staunch defenders of Protestantism. Events in England soon led to the overthrow of the despised royal governor Sir Edmund Andros. Politics, however, did not overly concern John. On 6 May 1689 a son Samuel had been born. With an ever growing young family, John's cares were more economic and familial than political. Living in a town with its face set to the sea John wisely chose to become the first New England Adams to turn his back on the land and go voyaging. "Captain" Adams did well.

Sometime in 1691 or 1692 Hannah had another child, Abijah. Both the child and the mother died. Although grief stricken, a widowed father needed a wife. John shortly married Hannah Checkley, a fortunate choice. The daughter of a distinguished family, she helped the captain inch up a notch in Boston society. In the first seven years of their marriage, she delivered five additional children, three of whom survived infancy.

Samuel's childhood was ordinary. In a world where mothers and their infants often died, there was nothing unusual about having a stepmother and a flock of step siblings. At home his stepmother taught him and the others rudiments of reading and writing. He may even have attended grammar school, but he never attended college. He was, however, blessed with good health, good family, and a talent for making money. Following the disastrous fire of 1711, Adams took advantage of a low real estate market and bought a house and lot on Purchase Street not far from the waterfront and overlooking the harbor. He may well have bought the property to convince Richard Fifield that he was a suitable husband for Fifield's daughter Mary. If so, it worked, and the year following Samuel and Mary were wed. In the same year, Fifield, a widower also, married Maria Mather, daughter of Increase Mather and sister to the renowned Cotton. The senior Samuel Adams was linked now to the most prominent family in the Bay Colony. Through these family connections he was part of an elaborate and large personal network that stretched into nearly every aspect of society.

Samuel and Mary settled into a conventional lifestyle. In their town, conversation and concerns pivoted around the arrival of ships, news from abroad, worries about weather, and neighborhood gossip. The Adamses saw life through the prism of their Puritan traditions, governed by a stern God whose hand had guided their ancestors across a "vast and furious" ocean to create a Zion in the wilderness.

Faith in the sureness of God's care over them buoyed Samuel and Mary through difficult times. In their 34 years of marriage, they celebrated the birth of 12 children but buried 9. In the family Bible Samuel recorded these moments of joy and grief.

Samuel and Mary's losses were daunting, even for eighteenth-century Boston. Faced with such unrelenting reminders of mortality, the elder Adams took special care to instruct his children in the matters he held dear—faithfulness to God and service to the community. That he placed such particular value on religion and community was hardly surprising. A descendant of the Puritan men and women who had first settled

Massachusetts, he may as a child even have known some of the first settlers, ancient and respected relics. His connection to the Mathers made him even more conscious of the momentous events that had brought his family to this place.

Puritans were serious about their lives and their mission. Indeed, they derived their name from their desire to "purify" the English church. They were well aware that humans are incapable of earthly perfection, which did not prevent them from striving toward that goal. They held strong notions of right and wrong, taken primarily from the Old Testament. They knew that damnation was always a possibility. Convinced as they were of their own righteousness, they did not welcome dissenting views, since to do so was to entertain error. Yet these characteristics were confined to neither Puritanism nor the seventeenth century. Powerful people who believed they held the monopoly on truth were likely to be intolerant toward others in any age.

Yet if the Puritans brought the dark side of the seventeenth century to Boston they also brought hope, as well as a sense of destiny. In the summer of 1630, as their fleet approached Boston, Gov. John Winthrop summoned the leaders of the expedition to join him aboard the flagship *Arbella*. He spoke to them about their mission. He told his brethren that "the work we have in hand, it is by mutual consent, through a special overruling providence and a more than an ordinary approbation of the churches of Christ, to seek out a place of cohabitation and consortship, under a due form of government both civil and ecclesiastical." In this community, "the care of the public must oversway all private respects by which not only conscience but mere civil policy doth bind us; for it is a true rule that particular estates cannot subsist in the ruin of the public." Winthrop commanded that all "rejoice together, mourn together, labor and suffer together—always having before our eyes our commission and community in the work, our community as members of the same body." He proclaimed, "we shall be as a city upon a hill, the eyes of all people are upon us." Winthrop was sincere in urging his fellow Puritans to hold dear to their communitarian, indeed utopian, views. The first settlers of Boston well understood that they were engaged in an effort that transcended the tiny settlement on the Shawmut peninsula. They were in a covenant with the Lord to preserve his ways so they might be a light to a corrupt world.

"Covenant" was a concept the Puritans borrowed from the Old Testament. Moses's Ten Commandments were the first covenant, or agreement. By those commandments the Lord gave to Moses and his people directions about the conduct of life. As long as they obeyed his commandments the Lord blessed Moses and his followers. When they disobeyed them he brought punishment. According to the Puritans, the New Testament was a new covenant, and the Lord demanded that his people obey its precepts. Since people were naturally sinful, that is, they would stray from obeying the covenant, it was the duty of government to make and enforce laws that kept people from sin.

Good government, led by good men, would produce a virtuous society, a community where morality and right action prevailed. Governments that supported virtue were to be supported by the people. If, on the other hand, the government and its leaders did not support morality and virtue, then the people had an obligation to dissolve it and seek better rulers. Winthrop and his associates had chosen not to dissolve the wicked government of England, but rather to preserve the covenant they held dear and bring it to Boston where it might be nurtured for a time in the future when others might look to Boston for leadership.

Good intentions notwithstanding, Boston quickly developed in directions troubling to Winthrop. Strangers arrived, brewing dissent and making conflict inevitable. Governance of the town, at first conducted as a part of church polity, gradually evolved in more secular dimensions. Matters once decided within the confines of the church meeting gradually moved onto the agenda of an increasingly separate body—the town meeting.

Concerned with problems of weights and measures, garbage in the streets, schools and taxes, the town meeting left issues of salvation and the interpretation of Holy Scripture to the church and its ministers. However, the two constitutions remained linked inasmuch as church membership was a necessary qualification for the right to vote in town meeting. As ever more "strangers" entered Boston, and insisted on a voice in civil matters, the town meeting struggled to accommodate them while still paying due deference to the role of the clergy and religion.

With little difficulty, the town meeting assumed authority over secular affairs, abetted by the colony government. In March 1631, for example, the General Court granted "every Towne within this Pattent" responsibility to ensure that all men "except magistrates and ministers" be "furnished with good and sufficient armes." This responsibility was only the first of many delegated, and within a relatively short time towns emerged as the colony's single most important governing unit. When the court attempted to rein in or subvert town authority it was likely to meet fierce resistance. In the winter of 1656, the court appointed a committee to adjudicate a particularly virulent dispute among the people of Sudbury. When the court's delegation arrived, the townspeople quickly put aside their own differences, and told the visitors that insofar as an issue pertained to the town, "We shall be judged by men of our own choosing." Every town of the colony echoed Sudbury's views.

In Boston, participation in town affairs had been limited to men admitted freemen of the colony, that is, adult males who owned property and were members of the Puritan church. Before the end of the first decade, those restrictions, in practice and law, had been relaxed. In 1647 the General Court took "into consideration the useful . . . abilities of divers inhabitants amongst us, which are not freemen, which, if improved to publick use, the affaires of this common wealth may be the easier carried on in the severall townes." To bring these persons into the body politick, it ruled that the "inhabitants" may "have their vote in the choyce of select men for towne affaires, assessment of rates, and other prudentials proper." The court's largesse merely enacted what was already common in practice. Within a few years the number of voters in Boston increased dramatically. Given such broad participation, the town meeting grew more vocal and powerful, arousing suspicions. In 1655 a committee of the General Court reported in horror that Boston's town meeting had gone far beyond the bounds of propriety to a point where "Scotch servants, Irish negers and persons under one and twenty years" not only attended sessions but actually voted.

While certain members of the court railed at Boston's boldness, they were powerless to reverse the trend. At the call of the constable each March, the annual town meeting convened. As the men filed into the meeting chamber, no one scrutinized their qualifications; indeed, participation in the meeting may well have extended beyond what the law allowed. First, the meeting elected officers for the year. Most important were the selectmen, whose task it was to conduct town affairs when the meeting was not in session. In addition to the selectmen were several standing committees that oversaw schools, health, safety, and roads. When necessary, special committees attended to particular issues. Agendas could be lengthy, and business sometimes requiring several meetings could trail off into the spring.

Whatever its flaws (on more than one occasion the raucous sessions verged out of control, and they never allowed women to vote), the Boston town meeting was extraordinary. Such broad and open participation made it the most democratic institution in the British empire. Officials in London initially took no notice of its sturdy independence. They did, however, take careful and critical note of the colony's apparent political course, which seemed increasingly to be in conflict with the wider interests of the empire. These concerns came to a head in 1684, when the colony's original charter of 1629, a document that granted the settlers wide latitude, was revoked and replaced in 1691 by one far more restrictive. Henceforth the governor would no longer be elected by the freemen but appointed by the king. He, and not the General Court, as had previously been the case, would appoint the judicial, military, and administrative officers in the counties. He would also have veto power over acts of the legislature and the upper house, which had hitherto been elected by the voters, and would now be chosen by the lower house with the approval of the governor. The franchise too was altered. No longer would church membership be required for voting in provincial elections. Instead, a new provision stipulated that all freemen must either pay 40 shillings a year in taxes or hold personal property valued at £40. "In a few short paragraphs the charter had reduced popular participation in government, legislative rights, representation, consent and responsibility to a bare minimum . . . the king replaced the voters as sovereign constitutional authority, ultimate judge and dominant political power in Massachusetts."

Ironically, the charter that so altered the colony's form of government made no mention whatsoever of town government. Had they been better informed and more alert, the king's ministers would undoubtedly have turned their attention to a "reform" of local government as well.

Instead, their lopsided effort to control the Bay Colony produced a thoroughly unintended result: "Royalizing" power at the provincial level enhanced the Boston town meeting. With the king and his minions holding sway at the top, popular politics centered on town meetings, with none more important than that governing the province's capital. "Preservation of the town meeting was absolutely essential to offset the new restrictions on popular participation and responsibility in the province government." Both local and popular, the town meeting reaffirmed its role as the voice of the people, whereas the province government, with its ties to London and its dependence upon the king's grace, distanced itself. The two bodies, seeking to govern the same community, but with different sources of power, were bound to collide.

Elisha Cooke was among the first town meeting members to sense the threat from the province. He led the Boston faction in the General Court and managed, by a series of clever stratagems, to preserve many of the powers of the town meeting. It was Cooke, for example, who devised a way by which the electorate in the town was expanded so as to encompass those most likely to support him. Province law required that town voters have a "£20 rateable estate." If enforced this would have meant that barely 200 of Boston's 1000 adult males could qualify to vote. Cooke's solution was to redefine "rateable estate." In previous years the "rateable estate" was considered to be the annual income or rent collected from property. Should this continue few townsmen would be eligible to vote. Cooke managed to secure a condition that henceforth "rateable estate" would be calculated by having the selectmen or tax commissioner multiply the rent or income by six. By this device the number of men qualifying increased geometrically. Nor was it any coincidence that Elisha Cooke himself was elected tax commissioner. Under his leadership popular town government thrived.

Upon his death in 1715, Cooke's son, Elisha Jr., crafted an even stronger faction. With Cooke in the chair these men, about twenty in number, met in the north end of Boston in a room heavy with the odor of good port and Virginia tobacco. In private, they laid "their plans for introducing certain persons into places of trust and power." Samuel Adams the elder was among those who caucused with Elisha Cooke.[1]

Elisha Cooke, Jr. and the elder Adams were strange bedfellows. Cooke had a well-deserved reputation for heavy drinking and carousing; Adams, on the other hand, shared

---

[1]The term *caucus* may well have originated in this context. Cooke's meetings took place in Boston's North End, the town center for shipbuilding. The Caulkers' Club was a local organization that sympathized with Cooke's faction, and Cooke may well have used the Caulkers' Club as a meeting place.

those traits often associated with his more famous son—sobriety, seriousness, dedication to religious principles, and hard work. Indeed, Adams was a deacon of the Old South, his mother's church, which he had joined in 1706. Whatever personal differences stood between these two men paled, however, in comparison to their shared devotion to the interests of Boston.

As a loyal member of the caucus, Adams played an important role in town politics. His service did not go unrewarded. He was chosen a justice of the peace, selectman, and representative to the General Court. Through his broad involvement in church and town affairs, he developed a wide circle of friends. His home was a bustling place where people often came to discuss the business of the town.

As visitors trooped through the house, young Samuel received an education he had yet to appreciate. At dinner he was bored by talk of London, land speculation, war, and politics. When the meal was finished and the men retired to their port and tobacco, Samuel was sent to bed, where he could lie quietly listening to muted voices speaking of places far away and of men whose names he did not know. Someday Samuel would sit at the table and engage in conversation on these weighty topics, but for the time being his main concern was school.

Like many young Boston boys, Samuel learned the basics of reading and writing from his mother. A pious woman, Mary Fifield taught her children from biblical texts. She did her job well. When Samuel was about 6, he sought admission to Boston Latin School.

On a summer afternoon, in the company of his father, he walked the few blocks from home, up Cotton Hill to the school. There they met the master Nathaniel Williams, a grizzled veteran, graduate of Harvard in 1693. Ordained in 1698 Williams shortly thereafter took up a church in Barbados. The sojourn in the West Indies ruined his health, and he returned to Boston, where in 1703 the selectmen appointed him master at the Latin School. Williams, however, never fully recovered, and barely a year after his appointment, he claimed ill health and offered his resignation. Fearful of losing their distinguished teacher, the selectmen offered to hire an assistant if he would remain. Williams agreed. On the day Samuel Adams entered the school, Williams's assistant, or usher, was John Lovell, Harvard class of 1728. For five years Lovell served as usher, until finally in 1734, Williams, his health beyond repair, officially resigned. By unanimous vote, the selectmen named Lovell the new master.

For 41 years Lovell reigned on School Street, retiring only in 1775, when his Tory leanings made life in Boston uncomfortable. On the day momentous events were reported from Lexington and Concord, he is reputed to have dismissed his students by telling them, "War's begun and school's done: *Deponite libros*" (Put down your books). In his four decades of service, Lovell trained more than two thousand of Boston's best and brightest boys. As one observer noted, "Lovell's school with its hot stove and its hundred steaming greatcoats was part of the indelible memories of a long generation of Boston men."

Like the two dozen or so boys who presented themselves for admission, Samuel read a few verses from the King James Bible. Thanks to his mother's many hours of instruction, Samuel performed the task with ease. Having established his literacy—the family background spoke for itself—he was admitted to Latin School.

At seven each morning Lovell tugged on the bell rope to announce the day's commencement. The school itself, an old wooden structure built back at the turn of the century, was hardly impressive. Crammed onto a small lot just behind the Anglican church, it was two stories high, about 40 feet wide where it faced the street, and 25 feet deep. Inside the boys were grouped at benches according to their age.

The curriculum was fixed and had not changed in decades. Lovell, who did most of the teaching, drilled students in their lessons. Among the lazy, recalcitrant, or slow, the "Old Gaffer," as he was called by his students, roamed, ferule at the ready. According to one alumnus, the implement "was a short, stubbed, greasy-looking article, which, when not in use, served him as a stick of sugar candy. The lightest punishment was one clap, the severest four and the most usual, two—one on each hand." Given Lovell's Tory leanings (he joined the Loyalist exodus to Halifax in March 1776), it is not surprising that on reflection many years after leaving the school, his Whiggish students saw in the master's behavior elements of "barbarism" and "oppression" common to the king's followers. In fact, Lovell's pedagogy was typical of the time, and his students, while fearing him, saw nothing unusual in his classroom style.

At his bench, Samuel hunched over his Greek and Latin texts, including such standbys as Aesop's *Fables*, Eutropius's *Roman History*, and Ward's *Lily's Grammar*. How well, or poorly, Samuel did at Latin School is unknown. In one of his books he made a marginal note about the value of learning exceeding riches; given his later career, it seems reasonable to assume that the sentiment was genuine.

The narrow curriculum provided for no frills. The purpose of Latin School was to prepare students in the tradition of the liberal arts so that they could follow the same path at college. Classical languages were the key to the wisdom of the ancients, as well as knowledge of history, philosophy, and natural science.

Of course, school did not occupy every minute of Samuel's childhood. He had Thursday and Saturday afternoons off as well as Sunday. For some portion of his time, he probably assisted his father in the family business of preparing and selling malt, a product in demand for cooking and brewing. But even that must have left moments for other diversions. In good weather, Samuel may have walked the short distance down to the docks, where he could fish, swim, or just lollygag watching vessels move in and out of the harbor and listening to sailors swap lies. In the winter, sledding was great fun, pushing off from atop Beacon Hill, and, with a loud hullo, he could race down School Street, past Latin, and practically to the water's edge. If the weather was cold enough, there might be skating on Frog Pond.

In the spring of 1736, shortly before school ended, Samuel and his father took the ferry across the Charles River and made their way to Cambridge. It was time for the admission interview with the president of Harvard. All prospective students were required to present themselves to the president and the college tutors for examination. The college laws of 1734 stated the requirements: the ability "to read, construe and parse Tully, Virgil, or Such like common Classical Latin Authors; and to write true Latin in Prose, and to be Skill'd in making Latin verse, or at Least in the rules of Prosodia; and to read, construe and parse ordinary Greek, as in the New Testament, Isocrates, or such like, and decline the Paradigms of Greek Nouns, and Verbs."

Samuel had no difficulty gaining entrance. His Latin School preparation, a good pedigree, and his father's social status all guaranteed acceptance. He entered with the class of 1740, "twenty-three strong." Barely 14 he was one of the youngest members of the class. Rank in class, determined by the student's family status, put him sixth—a tribute to his father's prominence in Boston affairs.

CHAPTER 2

Harvard and Home

❖
❖

Adams's Harvard was a pleasant and comfortable place. Since 1725 the college had been under the guidance of President Benjamin Wadsworth, class of 1690. For three decades Wadsworth was the pastor of the first (often contentious) church of Boston, and had encountered ample opportunities to hone the political skills necessary for a successful college presidency. His critics accused him of being a trimmer in all matters; those taking a kinder view considered him conciliatory. The Harvard corporation liked what it saw in Wadsworth and settled a generous salary on him as well as a dwelling, eventually to be called Wadsworth House, which still graces Harvard Yard today.

In the fall of 1736 President Wadsworth welcomed the 23 members of the class of 1740. Adams's classmates, all from Massachusetts, were a relatively undistinguished lot. According to college practice, incoming students were ranked by their family's standing in the colony. The ordering principles were as follows: (1) sons of the governor of the colony, (2) lieutenant governor, (3) members of the governor's council, (4) justices of the peace by date of commission, (5) sons of alumni, and (6) the rest, generally about half the class, by intellectual promise. Adams's class had no one in the first three rankings, and in

February 1737, when the order was posted, Adams, son of a justice of the peace, ranked sixth.

Altogether slightly fewer than one hundred undergraduates in all four years were enrolled in the college that fall. Although a few students were granted permission to board elsewhere, most lived in Massachusetts Hall. Completed in 1720, Massachusetts Hall was one of three buildings that made up the college. Directly across from Massachusetts was Harvard Hall; to the east was Stoughton; and the incomplete quadrangle opened to the west.

After being assigned to a chamber with a number of other "chums," Adams settled into the college routine. Tutor for the class was Daniel Rogers, Harvard 1725. His task was to instruct in all subjects. One of his fellow tutors referred to him as an "ignorant dolt." Dolt or not, Rogers took Adams and his classmates through a curriculum that placed a heavy emphasis on logic, metaphysics, ethics, natural philosophy, mathematics, geography, astronomy, rhetoric, elocution, and composition. Classic texts were the source of much of this wisdom, and Adams, along with his peers, undoubtedly took instruction in Latin, Greek, and Hebrew.

But in addition to the ancients Adams also learned about more contemporary writers and philosophers such as John Locke and James Harrington. The events of the Glorious Revolution and the rise of Parliament had spawned a tidal wave of discussion about the relationship of power, liberty, government, and the right of revolution. Adams nodded quick agreement with Locke's assertion that the goal of good government was to ensure men rights to life, liberty, and property. While based on more secular concerns, Locke's concept of the covenant between government and citizens was parallel to Adams's own deep-seated commitment to the covenant of his ancestors.

Adams's day began at six with morning prayer. Breakfast followed, a meal students provided for themselves. Much to the annoyance of the president and the tutors, Adams and his chums took this requirement as an invitation to organize breakfast parties, some of which stretched toward noon. A disgruntled president was forced to decree that no one could breakfast after 9 A.M.

Following breakfast Adams listened to lectures. At midday dinner, served in a common area, students and faculty sat down together, although at separate tables. Afternoons were occupied with meetings and recitations in company with Tutor Rogers. After supper, which were usually leftovers from dinner, students were expected to retire to their chambers for study.

Despite the best efforts of the president and tutors, Harvard could be a raucous place. The chief engine of mischief was alcohol. Despite rules banning spirits, resourceful students found ways to smuggle liquor into their rooms. Carrying boldness to the very edge of danger, some clever students even managed to brew beer in their chambers. For most, however, it was far simpler to venture out beyond the yard where there were always ample supplies to fuel "drinking frolics." Certain days were more troublesome than others. Eighteenth-century Massachusetts had few holidays. The various religious feasts common in England were discouraged in a colony still living under the psychological force of Puritanism. Perhaps it was the lack of holidays that made the few available occasions so vividly celebratory.

There were two great moments of release. Chanting "Remember, remember the fifth of November, gunpowder, treason, and plot," students marched through the yard on Guy Fawkes Day tearing up fences, even the president's, and stacking up the boards for a bonfire. Annual warnings issued by the president had no effect.[1] Guy Fawkes Day, however, paled in comparison to the fury let loose at commencement, usually a Wednesday in July. As the time drew near for receiving their

---

[1]On November 5, 1605, a group of Catholic conspirators attempted to blow up Parliament. Guy Fawkes was among them. The plot was discovered and the conspirators arrested. Several of them, including Fawkes, were eventually executed.

degrees, which would soon put them beyond the reach of college authorities, students cast off restraint. Presidents railed against the drunkenness and disorder and promulgated rules from prohibiting drinking in rooms to banning rum cakes. All to no avail.

Commencement was not just an occasion for hilarity in the yard but a colonywide event that brought together "all the cheap-jacks, Indian medicine men, acrobats and public entertainers, that New England afforded." For several days the tents of visitors littered Cambridge Common. According to one wag, "The Town's a cage fill'd with each kind of Bird."

In exasperation President Wadsworth decided on one occasion to keep the date of commencement a secret so no one could make preparations; on another he moved the event from Wednesday to Friday in the hope that the entire week would not be taken up in bacchanalia. Nothing worked. Students continued their best efforts to "Drink Harvard dry." Fines were levied, ears boxed, students "degraded," and finally expelled. Nothing seemed to work and at times the faculty records convey a sense of desperation as the authorities sought to stem the tide of vice.

In the midst of such a swelling sea, Adams remained an island of virtue. Only once between 1736 and 1740 did his name appear among the list of miscreants. In March he, Samuel Downe, and George Bethune, all Boston boys, were fined 5s each for "drinking prohibited liquors." Adams's record of virtue is either a tribute to his pious upbringing or proof of his skill at avoiding detection. We will never know which.

Near the end of Adams's freshman year, President Wadsworth died. As usual the choice of a successor devolved into a political and philosophical struggle. The Old Guard held tenaciously to orthodox Calvinism and insisted that the president do the same. Moderates were inclined toward a person of more liberal learning and attitudes. The debate came to a head during a private dinner party hosted by Gov. Jonathan Belcher. Concerned about the political implications of the selection process, Belcher chanced to ask his old friend John Barnard, minister in Andover, what he thought of Edward Holyoke. Belcher had heard some unkind comments about Holyoke and valued Barnard's opinion. Barnard told His Excellency that Holyoke was as orthodox a Calvinist as any man, though "too much of a gentleman, and of too catholic a temper, to cram his principles down another man's throat." A convinced and delighted Belcher declared, "Then I believe he must be the man." Belcher's endorsement swept Holyoke into office.

For Adams and his classmates, Holyoke's appointment was a gift. While in his heart he may well have been an orthodox Calvinist, in his public demeanor he proved to be both liberal and tolerant. During his presidency an entire generation of Massachusetts revolutionaries passed through Harvard including Samuel and John Adams, John Hancock, James Otis, Joseph Warren, and a flock of lesser lights. Undoubtedly Holyoke shared with these young men his views on government. He may well have told them, as he once publicly told the governor himself, "All forms of government originate from the People; that is, God in his Providence hath influenced them; some to fix upon one Form of Government, and some upon another. As these forms then have originated from the People, doubtless they may be changed whensoever the Body of them choose to make such an alteration."

Holyoke was wise enough to couch his liberal views in ways that never directly challenged the more orthodox tenets of the corporation and overseers. He, like most of the faculty and students, drifted along on a gentle liberal tide. Their God was not the wrathful Jehovah, saving some and condemning others, but a gentle, kind, and loving father. While their covenant still meant surrendering to the will of God, it did not mean resignation and inaction. Holyoke preached the possibility of change and the rule of man in shaping his own destiny. Adams and his chums heeded the lesson.

As spring 1740 crept into summer, Adams and his classmates prepared for the orgy of commencement. As usual Holyoke and other authorities, ever hopeful for a decorous occasion, issued stern warnings about improper behavior. They need not have worried, for fate intervened to forestall the event. In June Cambridge was struck by throat distemper (diphtheria). On the twenty-third of that month Holyoke's son William died. That same day the president ordered the college closed and the students sent home.

At a time when all should have been joy and anticipation, Adams's homecoming was covered with a pall. Having left melancholy in Cambridge he arrived in Boston to join his family in mourning over the death of his infant sister Mehetable, another victim of the throat distemper.

Samuel's grief was compounded by anxiety over his future. He was 17 and held a bachelor's degree. What next? According to family tradition, "the investigation of theology had much occupied his thoughts." If so, it is hardly surprising. Much the same could be said of any eighteenth-century graduate of Harvard College. In Adams's case, however, theology was not the focus of attention. Politics and business were far more intriguing to him than biblical explication. During his years in Cambridge he kept in close touch with his family and friends at home and had followed affairs in Boston with keen interest.

Boston was in trouble. Since the early 1730s her economy had been stagnant. Restrictions placed on the importation of foreign molasses by Parliament's Act of 1733 had depressed not only local distilling but the associated industries of shipbuilding and fishing as well. In 1720 Boston shipyards had launched 40 vessels. In 1740 barely 20 hulls slid into the water. The town experienced rampant unemployment. Those who could left; those who remained suffered.

Confronted with such dire circumstances, further colored by the news in 1739 that France and Great Britain were once again at war, the elder Adams and his fellow Bostonians sought ways to bolster the economy. One of the chief restraints on trade was the insufficient supply of gold and silver. Since at least 1691 the provincial government had attempted to alleviate its nagging currency problem by issuing paper money. Its uses and circulation were, however, generally limited. The issuance of 1691, for example, had been designated to pay for Gov. William Phips's unsuccessful expedition against Canada. The law allowed the government to issue paper money, which it then accepted back in payment of taxes. In the meantime, before its return to the province treasury, the paper could circulate as currency. Although conservative merchants, whose faith was firmly planted in silver and gold, were uneasy with the government's decision to print money, they were consoled by the restricted amount and duration of the issuance.

Conservative misgivings notwithstanding, paper money became a popular means of public finance not only in Massachusetts but in neighboring colonies as well. As more paper currency circulated, its value grew uncertain. Royal governors, Massachusetts included, were therefore ordered to curb the issuance. Private individuals were not so constrained. In October 1739 John Colman and 395 others, prominent among them Deacon Samuel Adams, put forth a plan to float bills secured by real estate, just the sort of scheme abhorred by the governor and conservative merchants, for it would put in circulation bills whose value could be unstable, but which creditors might nonetheless be asked to accept. Such a scheme favored debtors who through this plan might find a way to repay old debts in new depreciated money. For the moment, however, there was nothing the governor could do. Colman's proposal was perfectly legal, and on 10 March a broadside appeared about town announcing that anyone who wished to subscribe to the land bank could present himself at the Exchange Tavern in King Street. A subscription conferred membership in the company and the right to vote on company affairs. The only payment required was 40s per £1000 for organizational expenses. Adams and the other investors put up mortgages as security and promised to pay an annual interest of 3 percent. In return, they received paper bills in the amount they had secured. These bills could then circulate.

People flocked to King Street. Within a short time, at least a thousand individuals from all over the province had borrowed money, all of whom expected their fellow land bank partners, as well as others, to accept their notes as valid payment for goods or services received.

Whatever its economic merits or demerits, the land bank was enormously popular. It was also somewhat democratic inasmuch as individual holdings tended to be small and widely distributed. The company elected nine directors, among them Deacon Adams, to manage affairs. At first the bank's opponents tried to create their own bank, based on silver. While popular in the upper chamber, the measure was decidedly unpopular in the House, where several leaders were directors of the bank and a great number of representatives were investors.

In a rather foolish move, the governor insisted that the House investigate the bank. That intimation of illegality was seen as a veiled threat, and the House refused to conduct the inquiry. Belcher was furious. Determined to kill "so vile a scheme," he forbade all those in the province holding a commission under his seal to support the land bank. The command produced a flood of resignations, including one from Deacon Samuel Adams, who held a commission as a justice of the peace. Outraged at Adams and his associates, Belcher ignored their resignations and instead dismissed them.

The governor went even further. Letters were sent to the registers of deeds in the counties asking them to supply the names of all individuals holding land bank mortgages. Colonels of the militia were ordered to report on their officers' attitudes toward the bank. Clearly Belcher and his allies, among the most prominent the Boston merchant Thomas Hutchinson, were taking an extreme view. The land bank cause was rapidly escalating into an issue of rights.

Furious at such tactics Henry Lee of Worcester wrote to Belcher. Lee was firm:

> I am determined to do what I can to encourage it [the land bank], and think that the privilege of an Englishman is my sufficient warrant therefor. As I act to my conscience, I regard being punished any way for differing in my opinion from the Council to be a civil persecution, and to be de-

prived of my office until I be proved unfaithful in it, or have violated the laws of the land, I look on as an invasion of my native rights.

Determined to kill the monster, the council, at the urging of Belcher and some Boston merchants, took its own stand. On 27 January 1741 the council issued an order that no attorney in any way associated with the land bank could appear before it. This was a harsh blow because at the time the council presided over all probate matters. Any lawyer involved in the land bank was now banned from that lucrative practice.

Flailing away at minor officials, lawyers, and anyone else connected with the land bank proved futile. Given its strong base of popular support, the bank easily withstood assaults from the governor and council. Several towns, in open defiance of the royal government, accepted land bank notes as tax payment. In Bristol County rumors spread that an armed mob was preparing to march on Boston to demand that certain merchants friendly to the governor be forced to exchange the corn they were storing for land bank notes.

If the bank could not be killed from within the colony then it might be killed from without. From the outset, Belcher had kept his London superiors well informed about the progress of the bank. He turned to London for the ultimate remedy. In the spring of 1741 Parliament passed "An Act for restraining and preventing several unwarrantable schemes and undertakings in his Majesty's Colonies and Plantations in America."

Measures that had proved too weak in Boston gained sufficient strength in London. The bank was dead. The act stipulated that the directors were liable for any notes presented to the bank for payment in gold or silver. If payment was not immediately forthcoming the plaintiffs could appeal to the courts, which were authorized to award treble damages.

Lacking much of a fortune, Deacon Adams found himself hounded in the courts. Special commissions were appointed to inquire and make recommendations. In 1747 a fire destroyed all the bank records, but the suits persisted. The deacon died in 1748, but the suits did not, and so the court attached his estate.

Indeed, not until 1768 did the matter end. By that time most of the litigants were either dead or exhausted and both the royal governor and the House of Representatives were embroiled in other affairs.

For young Samuel, fresh out of Harvard, the land bank quarrel was a wonderful introduction to Boston politics. Almost as soon as the newly minted college graduate returned to the family home, his father arranged for him to work in the countinghouse of Thomas "Death's Head" Cushing. The unkind nickname was attached to Cushing by Governor Belcher who remarked on the man's wan visage. Cushing was a prominent merchant, politician, and lawyer in the town. Like Samuel's father, he was an ally of Elisha Cooke, and in fact, he succeeded Cooke as moderator of the town meeting. He also served in the House of Representatives, eventually becoming speaker. Deacon Adams had high hopes that Cushing's influence assured Samuel a career in either law or business.

From his perch in Cushing's countinghouse as well as the family home on Purchase Street, Adams could closely observe ongoing political battles. His father's enemies became his enemies, his father's friends his friends. He watched how the deacon, Colman, Cushing, and others maneuvered and managed votes in town meeting and the House. He saw how important it was to build coalitions with the country towns, and he learned that the best way to reach them was through newspapers. He also came to the understanding that his community was split between those whose sentiments, faith, and loyalty rested within the confines of the colony and town, and those who, when pressed, abandoned local attachments and appealed directly to a distant and increasingly alien power in London.

As the land bank issue slowly wound to its conclusion, Samuel Adams returned to Harvard for a graduate degree. In awarding the master's degree Harvard followed the English tradition. Three years after receipt of the bachelor's degree, candidates returned to campus and were asked to make a formal response to a philosophical question in which they drew on their undergraduate preparation as well as their reading and experience since commencement. Following neatly in the tradition Adams presented himself for his degree in the spring of 1743.

It cannot be a coincidence that the question he chose to address was, "Is it Lawful to resist the Supreme Magistrate, if the Commonwealth cannot otherwise be preserved?" Candidate Adams argued in the affirmative, presumably viewing the "Supreme Magistrate" as king and Parliament and the "Commonwealth" as his town and province.

"Death's Head" Cushing and Deacon Adams were not the sort of individuals apt to pay much attention to young Samuel's theoretical disputation. They were practical men of affairs thoroughly committed to what they viewed as the ongoing battle to preserve the rights of popular government (i.e., the town meeting and the provincial House of Representatives) against the encroachments of the royal governor and his allies.

By the time Adams settled himself back in Cushing's office, it was clear, despite his father's hopes, that neither law nor business attracted him. It was politics that excited Samuel. Recognizing his young charge's talents, Cushing admitted that "though active enough in mind and body, he would never do for a merchant; his whole soul was engrossed in politics." Samuel soon left Cushing's employ.

Deacon Adams's involvement in the land bank had been a political boon. In June 1746 he was elected to the House of Representatives; the following year he was elected to the council, only to be vetoed by the governor, a clear plus for Adams in Boston politics. But as the deacon's political star rose, his financial condition plummeted. Hectoring suits from the land bank drained his resources, but he did manage to raise £1000, a sum he loaned to his son to launch him in business.

As Cushing had warned, the loan proved a bad investment. The times were not favorable for new ventures. The demise of the land bank had left the colony in the hands of the hard money men who demanded payment in sound currency or silver, both of which were in short supply. Even astute merchants were having a difficult time surviving. Samuel, never good with money, was in over his head. Within a short time the deacon's money was gone, and Samuel was back home helping his father in the malt business and sampling Boston politics.

To the Adamses, father and son, politics was always more alluring than the dull business of preparing and selling malt. The deacon had stuck to the business out of necessity; young Samuel, with a Harvard education and his father's modest resources to fall back on, felt less compelled to follow that path. At the home on Purchase Street younger faces could now be seen at table, men of Samuel's generation mixing with the deacon and his associates, adding new voices to ongoing debates about liberty, Parliament, and taxes. These new voices, determined to seek wider audiences for their views, elected to use the press. Having honed his reasonable compositional skills at Harvard, Adams was eager to take a lead in this effort. Late in 1747 he and some of his friends formed a "club" whose purpose was to debate and write about public affairs. In January 1748 they found a ready outlet for their views in *The Independent Advertiser*, a newspaper published "at Queen Street near the prison" by Gamaliel Rogers and Daniel Fowle.

Although the *Advertiser* launched its first issue with the usual pious pronouncements that its pages were open "to whatever may be adapted to state and defend the rights and liberties of mankind," it was, in fact, in typical eighteenth-century English fashion, a highly partisan, univocal newspaper. The message was Whiggish and simple. The English constitution, based on the natural rights of man and manifested in common law, was a near perfect form of government. Adams wrote, "no form of civil government appears to me so well calculated to preserve this blessing, or to secure to its subjects all the most valuable advantages of civil society, as the English. In none that I have ever met with is the power of the governors and the rights of the governed more nicely adjusted."

Thus, with youthful exuberance, Adams expressed the joy of being an Englishman. Yet he was not just an Englishman; he was also a seventh-generation American. One hundred years of settlement and 3000 miles of ocean had provided ample opportunity for the people of Massachusetts to evolve their own variations of British constitutional government. Adams asserted that the colonial charter secured all the English liberties, in addition to other privileges which the common people of the mother country lacked. The Massachusetts settlers "had so severely felt the effects of tyranny and the weight of the bishop's yoke, that they underwent the greatest difficulties and toils to secure to themselves and transmit to their posterity those invaluable blessings; and we, their posterity, are this day reaping the fruits of their toils."

Steeped in the history of his own nation as well as sagas of a more distant past, Adams fully appreciated that liberty was a delicate flower. He believed, as did most Whig philosophers of his day, that political power like a raging lion was bent on devouring liberty. Governments, according to William Penn, were like clocks: Only man could set them in motion. Those men, if not virtuous, would be enemies to liberty and so too would their government.

That good government required good men was a commonplace in the eighteenth century, but for Adams that commonplace was invested with special meaning. His town had been founded on a commitment to mission and covenant. Boston was the "city upon a hill," where the common good took priority over private concerns. To be sure, in the century since its founding, much had changed. Outsiders could well scoff at any boast of Boston exceptionalism, but for Adams, government was a covenant bound by the sinews of virtue, and there could be no better example of such a government in the world or in history than that which ruled Massachusetts and Boston. "Happy beyond expression! in the form of our government, in the liberty we enjoy."

In the midst of their struggle to define the meaning of virtue, commitment, and covenant, Adams's generation found a model of selfless service in David Brainerd. Born into a large and well-known Connecticut family, Brainerd was orphaned at an early age. After failing as a farmer at age 20 he decided "to devote myself to the ministry; and imagined I did dedicate myself to the Lord." He entered Yale to prepare for his calling.

Brainerd's early years at Yale coincided with the Great Awakening. For years the churches of New England had been drifting away from the strict Calvinism of the early founders. In doctrine and in sermons "a rational and practical Christianity had emerged," a set of beliefs that recognized freedom of the will and the independence of the individual and even hinted at a Unitarian as opposed to a Trinitarian approach to God. Such liberal tendencies provoked a conservative reaction.

Itinerant preachers like George Whitefield and Gilbert Tennant, preaching stirring sermons of "hell and damnation," urged a return to fundamental tenets. Brainerd heard the message at Yale and took up the call. He criticized members of the college for their lack of religion, noting, for example, that tutor Chauncey Whittelsey had "no more grace than a Chair." On another occasion Brainerd was overheard wondering that Rector Thomas Clap "did not drop down dead." The authorities at liberal Yale were not amused. Brainerd was expelled.

Expulsion from Yale only fanned Brainerd's zeal. Eventually ordained by the New York presbytery in 1744 and supported by the Scottish Society for the Propagation of Christian Knowledge, Brainerd took charge of an Indian mission in New Jersey. It was an unhappy experience for Brainerd, and probably not much better for the Indians. Despite his efforts, he made few converts. At the same time the physical strain took a toll on his always fragile health. Sick and dying he went to Northampton, Massachusetts, in June 1747, to live out his last few weeks with the family of Jonathan Edwards, one of the most famous of the Great Awakening preachers. There Brainerd died on 9 October 1747.

Brainerd had kept a diary. After his death, Edwards saw in the young man's life an opportunity to demonstrate the remarkable providences of the Lord. By modern standards, Brainerd's diary entries recall the morose, self-tormented reflections of a man filled with the terrors of sin and of dying. At the same time, however, the work also portrays a person who against all obstacles, spiritual and secular, led an exemplary life in which, Edwards stressed, loyalty, virtue, and true commitment triumphed, even unto death.

Edwards's *Account of the Life of the Rev. Mr. David Brainerd* was published in Boston in 1749. Samuel Adams was one of its first subscribers. The young minister had earlier visited the town and spent some considerable time with several local gentlemen, Adams probably among them. In life, and certainly in death, David Brainerd was about as close to being a saint as any Bostonian would admit. To Adams, Brainerd represented the ideal person—virtuous, zealous, and unwavering, working out his own salvation through an extraordinary commitment to his community and little concern for his secular self. Adams saw in Brainerd the model for a life.

CHAPTER 3

Rumblings

❖
❖

Reading Edwards's *Life of Brainerd* and musing in print over the meaning of English liberties, laws, and constitutions were abstract diversions attractive to young people of good education. Walking the streets of the town, however, Adams witnessed the harsh reality of a community in distress.

Crushing the land bank had served the interests of creditors, but it further aggravated the chronic shortage of money, a burden falling most heavily on those in debt. As the war with France dragged on, higher taxes were levied for defense. French privateers ransacked the sea-lanes off New England, so that the prices of increasingly scarce imports rose while real wages fell. The number of Bostonians seeking public support climbed to new heights.

One of the trades laid low was distilling. For years Boston distillers had smuggled French molasses while customs officers winked. But what revenue laws had failed to check, war disrupted. Boston distillers groaned under a 50 percent decline in their business. Without the town's mainstay of West India trade, other businesses slumped. Shipbuilding nearly stopped altogether, and 25 of the town's butchers closed up shop and headed for the countryside. According to one estimate, between 1741 and 1746, the town's trade declined by at least

£200,000 or something in the neighborhood of £12 per capita. Since the average laborer was earning only 3 pence per day, the loss experienced by each and every household in the town was devastating.

While French depredations accelerated local grief, Boston's woes had been a long time coming. Indeed, its predicament could be traced back to its very origins.

From the outset, the port of Boston had looked eastward. A niggardly soil and stunted rivers penetrating only a few miles inland had forced the town's merchants to seek profits away and at sea rather than at home. With a skill born of necessity, Boston's merchants had danced around the Atlantic world shuttling vessels to the West Indies, the Carolinas, the Chesapeake, north to Nova Scotia, Newfoundland, and eastward to England. "Forsaking an unpromising hinterland, Boston's merchants instead pursued an aggressive expansion of their maritime foreland into the Atlantic economy."

That "unpromising hinterland" differed greatly from the bustling metropolis. Barely an afternoon's walk from Boston's Long Wharf, center for international trade, carried the ramblers among small nuclear villages that subsisted on farming, far closer in spirit to European peasant communities than to the cosmopolitan entrepôt Boston had become.

Dependence on an empirewide trading network and a dearth of local exports placed Boston in an exposed position. By the early eighteenth century, the town had already seen its once preeminent position on the Atlantic frontier deteriorate. Now it faced a dual challenge.

Philadelphia and New York and, to a lesser extent, Norfolk and Charleston had emerged as serious rivals. As these comparatively new ports gained strength and markets, their merchants undertook for themselves what the men of Boston had once done for them, that is, exported their raw materials and delivered imports. A second challenge surfaced when new trades developed. Beginning in the 1730s, rice from the Carolinas and wheat from the mid-Atlantic were booming commodities. Demand in Europe exploded, and the merchants of

Charleston, Philadelphia, and New York, ports nearby the growing areas, grabbed the new business. Bostonians were closed out.

As Boston's economy suffered, its vulnerabilities were unmasked. Left to their own devices, its hinterland neighbors had developed an economy and a culture not necessarily attuned to the great port. Differences that in good times might be glossed over, in bad times erupted into opposition on the battleground where the two sides most often engaged—the General Court. In the wider world Boston's addiction to international trade left it open to a less predictable source of grievance. Decisions made in London, over which Boston had little or no influence, could have a dramatic effect on the fortunes of the town.

Whether or not many Bostonians, if any, fathomed the underlying problems of the town, clearly they appreciated that war and hard money had caused them pain. Each year there were fewer and fewer taxpayers to fund the ever rising costs of town government. In 1738 there had been 3395 taxpayers. Barely five years later that number stood at 2972. Even more distressing was the fact that the burden had grown from £8,600 in 1738 to a crippling £12,000 at the later date. Nearly £4 each!

Borrowing was the only path out, and each year the selectmen arranged for loans on anticipated revenues. Each year they fell short, failed to pay on the principal, and so both principal and interest grew apace.

In the midst of this public misery, Samuel Adams suffered his own personal loss. After a brief illness Deacon Samuel Adams died on the morning of 8 March 1748. He left a widow and three children. The eldest was Mary, spouse to James Allen; Samuel was the middle child, and he was followed by a younger brother Joseph. As the eldest son, Samuel carried on the family business and continued to live on Purchase Street with his mother and younger brother.

Six months after the deacon's death, Boston welcomed the news of peace. The treaty of Aix-la-Chapelle ended King

George's war. Along with his fellow townsmen, Adams hoped that peace would renew prosperity. He was disappointed.

In the House of Representatives, hard money men with the support of members from outside Boston pushed through legislation basing local currency on silver. James Allen, a Boston representative and Adams's brother-in-law, denounced the measure. For his brazenness, he was expelled from the chamber. In December 1748 the voters returned him, but the House, still not satisfied, would not seat him until he had delivered an apology for his intemperate remarks. Having turned a deaf ear to Bostonians' entreaties for a more generous currency, the House, increasingly under the control of country elements, allotted province taxes in a manner that unfairly burdened the colony's largest town.

Adams, Allen, and their fellow townsmen felt abused and abandoned. First the royal governor and Parliament had destroyed the land bank, and now their own House seemed bent on sucking the town dry. At home, Adams undoubtedly spent many an evening over port and tobacco in long and heated conversation with Allen and others. It was no coincidence that within a few days of an evening meeting, a newspaper essay often appeared assailing Parliament's intrusions and calling on citizens to be wary lest they lose their rights. With "wit, ingenuity and profound argument," Adams and his friends strove to make life uncomfortable for those they considered political enemies.

At 27, and still a bachelor, Samuel Adams was beginning to stand apart. Indeed, he was one of only 4 in his Harvard class of 23 who remained unmarried. Not far from the Adams home, stood the Old South Church. Samuel's father, of course, had been a deacon of the church, and since its founding, the family's good friend Samuel Checkley had served as minister. As distinguished and well respected as the Reverend Mr. Checkley was, his wife Elizabeth Rolfe was probably better known, not only in Boston but throughout the province. When Reverend Checkley died in December 1769, newspaper obituaries devoted more space to describing his wife, who had died some years before, than to extolling his virtues and accomplishments.

Elizabeth Rolfe's claim to fame was that she had survived the infamous 1708 massacre at Haverhill, a town on the New Hampshire border about 30 miles north of Boston. One family historian described the event.

> [H]er father, mother, and a sister were massacred. When Mr. Rolfe heard the alarm he leaped from his bed, placed himself against the door, and called to the soldiers for assistance; but no assistance came. The enemy shot through the door and wounding Mr. Rolfe, he could no longer guard it. Retreating through his house he was followed and tomahawked near his well. The Indians then found Mrs. Rolfe and her youngest child, Mehitable. One of them sunk his hatchet deep into the mother's head, while another took the infant from her dying grasp, and dashed its head against a stone near the door. Two other daughters were taken into the cellar by Hagar, a negro servant, and placed under two tubs. She then hid herself behind some barrels. The enemy went into the cellar, passed and repassed the tubs, and even stepped upon a projecting foot of one of the children. They took meat from the barrels behind which Hagar was, drunk milk from the pans and then dashed them upon the bottom of the cellar, and finally left without discovering the trembling girls.

More than 60 years after the event, Elizabeth Rolfe's story continued to fascinate Boston.

The tale intrigued Samuel as well, but so too did Elizabeth's daughter, also named Elizabeth. Having known one another all their lives, Elizabeth and Samuel were married by her father on Tuesday evening, 17 October 1749. Whether by intention or not, with this marriage Samuel had joined one of the town's most distinguished families. To be sure, the alliance did not bring riches, but it did offer added respectability and fame.

Soon the children arrived, and they were often sickly. Their father now had less time for politics. The malt business, like other enterprises in the town, limped along in straitened circumstances, offering little but a bare maintenance.

Through the early 1750s, Boston and the country towns continued to rub against one another over money. Representatives from the countryside and friends of royal authority had little sympathy for the plight of the town. So apparent was Boston's distrust of the General Court that the town meeting went to the extraordinary measure of engaging a London agent to lobby Parliament directly. Differences notwithstanding, politics in the province seemed relatively calm for the moment. The story was much the same within Boston, where the town meeting caucus and the merchants seemed to have established a reasonable working relationship. Beyond Massachusetts, however, imperial affairs were in turmoil.

Few people in Boston, or elsewhere in the empire, were deceived by the peace of 1748. It was a truce, not a peace. England and France were irreconcilable. Wherever their boundaries touched, particularly in North America, sparks flew.

In June 1754 delegates from seven colonies, Massachusetts among them, met at Albany to discuss mutual defense against threats from the French and Indians. At the urging of Gov. William Shirley of Massachusetts and Thomas Hutchinson, and the subtle but incessant prodding of His Majesty's Commission of Trade and Plantations, the delegates framed a Plan of Union. The document was actually the handiwork of Pennsylvania delegate Benjamin Franklin. By its provisions, the plan called for "one General Government in America, including all the said Colonies."

Shirley and Hutchinson rode home to Boston carried along by hopes that the town and province would endorse the plan drawn at Albany. A skirmish between French and British forces had already taken place where the Allegheny and Monongahela Rivers joined. A Virginia militia colonel named George Washington, dispatched by Gov. Robert Dinwiddie to expel the French from the region, had failed in his mission and been repulsed. This news, auguring full-scale war, would, Shirley and Hutchinson believed, bring reason to the debate over the plan and open the eyes of all to the wisdom of uniting the colonies. They were wrong.

In Boston rumors about the Albany Plan caused more alarm than war whoops from the west. Having for years asserted its authority before with the General Court, the town had no intention of ceding any power whatsoever to some distant, vague body. Nor was the General Court about to consent to any plan that diminished its authority. On this issue, both the court and the town stood together. They rejected the Albany Plan.

There is no doubt about Adams's position. As a matter of principle, he opposed almost any initiative that might weaken town autonomy. Furthermore, having already witnessed, through the land bank debacle, what havoc a distant government could wreak, he had no intention of relinquishing the slightest iota of power. Nor did it escape Adams that Governor Shirley, whose hand had been heavy in suppressing the land bank, and Thomas Hutchinson, whose pleasure in striking at Adams father had been plain for all to see, were exponents of the plan. Whatever they endorsed, Adams was sure to oppose.

Washington's retreat from the Ohio marked the beginning of the final and epic struggle for control of colonial North America—the French and Indian War. From an imperial perspective, the war revealed all the weaknesses earlier identified at Albany: lack of coordination among colonies, bickering between military and civilian authorities, unprepared militia, and a host of regional and local petty jealousies. Notwithstanding internal squabbling the colonies did demonstrate a genuine harmony of objectives aimed at destroying French power in North America. Even in Boston, at least for the duration of the war, harmony became the hallmark of political deportment.

For Samuel Adams, however, private grief had shattered any comfort in tranquility. A little more than a year after their marriage, Samuel and Elizabeth had their first child, a son they named Samuel. He lived only 18 days. A year later a second son, also Samuel, was born and survived. Joseph, their third child, born on 23 June 1753, died two days later. Their first daughter, Mary, born exactly one year later on 23 June 1754, lived barely four months; their second daughter, Hannah, who entered the world on 21 January 1756, remained in it. Delivering five children, three deaths among them, took a heavy toll on Elizabeth. On 6 July 1757 she delivered a stillborn son. He would be the last child she would mourn. After struggling 19 days, Elizabeth died on 25 July. In the family bible Samuel recorded, "To her husband she was as sincere a Friend as she was a faithful Wife. Her exact economy in all other relative capacitys, her kindred on his side as well as her own admire. She ran her Christian race with a remarkable steadiness and finished in triumph. She left two small children. God grant they may inherit her graces!"

Hardly had Adams recovered from his grief over Elizabeth when the dead hand of the land bank rose up to strike him. As a director of the land bank, Samuel's father had remained vulnerable to litigation from those seeking to recover their investments. In the summer of 1758, the land bank had been moribund for 17 years, the elder Adams dead for 10. Nevertheless, the sheriff of Suffolk County declared his intention to seize the property of the deceased man and put it up for auction. The *Boston Newsletter* printed the notice that a public sale would take place

> at the Exchange Tavern in Boston To-morrow at noon. The Dwelling House, Malt-House, and other buildings with the Garden and lands adjoining, and the Wharf, Dock, and Flats before the same, being part of the estate of the late Samuel Adams, Esq. deceased, and is situated near Bull-Wharf, at the lower end of Summer Street in Boston aforesaid, the said estate being taken by warrant or execution under the hand and seal of the Hon. Commissioners for the more speedy finishing the Land Bank.

Never one to be cowed by authority, Adams defied the sheriff. Probably sympathetic with him in any case, Sheriff Greenleaf decided to defer the sale. Adams, granted some time, went public with his justification, carried in the *Newsletter*.

To Stephen Greenleaf, Esq.

> Sir I observe your Advertisement for the sale of the Es-
> tate of Samuel Adams, Esq., director of the Land Bank Com-
> pany. Your predecessor, Colonel Pollard, had the same affair
> in hand five years before his death; but with all his known
> firmness of mind, he never brought the matter to any con-
> clusion, and his *Precept*, I am told, is not returned to this
> Day. The reason was he, as well as myself, was advised by
> gentlemen of the law, that his proceeding was illegal and
> unwarrantable; and therefore he very prudently declined
> entering so far into this affair as to subject his own Estate to
> danger. How far your determination may lead you, you
> know better than I. I would only beg leave, with freedom, to
> assure you, that I am advised and determined to prosecute
> to the law any person whomsoever who shall trespass upon
> that Estate.

Adams meant what he said, and careful to have secured
the support of friends, he was able to raise enough of a ruckus
to forestall any sale of the family estate. As Thomas Hutchinson put it unkindly in the third volume of his *History of the
Colony of Massachusetts Bay and Province,* written after the Revolution, "by intimidating both the sheriff and those persons who
intended to purchase, he prevented the sale, kept the estate in
his possession, and the debt of the Land Bank unsatisfied."

In 1757 William Shirley stepped down as royal governor.
He had served in that post since 1741 and thus would be the
longest serving governor in the history of the colony. Disputes
notwithstanding, among them the land bank and the rejection
of the Albany Plan, Shirley had been a relatively popular governor. His departure was made palatable by the news that his re-
placement was Thomas Pownall, a man known to be even more
friendly to the interests of the colony. Upon his arrival in August 1757, Pownall was welcomed warmly, and he soon proved
to be even more popular than the fondly remembered Shirley.

Although short, lasting slightly under three years, Pownall's administration was an "era of good feeling." With war
raging against the French and Indians, the new governor well

understood the merits of cultivating good relations with the people of Boston and of Massachusetts. This he did with skill and tact. The French and Indian threat dampened internal dissent and the genial, accommodating Pownall achieved unprecedented harmony.

Controversial issues like the land bank receded into the background. There was less rancor in the town meeting, and the elected representatives to the General Court were seated without contest. Even the appointment of the unpopular Thomas Hutchinson as lieutenant governor in January 1758 failed to provoke a protest.

Those who equated harmony with deference, however, did so at their peril. Samuel Adams and other defenders of town prerogatives interpreted Pownall's agreeableness to be a validation of their deep-seated belief that the town meeting was the purest, most representative political body. Other bodies—at home, the General Court and at a greater distance, Parliament—performed valuable functions, but they were obligated to do so without violating the fundamental privileges of local government, for government closest to the people could best secure their rights and liberties.

Pownall's polite style and the success of British arms against the French persuaded the General Court to accede to the governor's requests for support. The requests were modest. English policy under prime minister William Pitt placed the heaviest burden on the people of Britain, thereby allowing the colonists to escape what many in England believed to be their responsibilities for financing wars in their quadrant. The fall of Quebec in 1759 and the capture of Montreal the following year proved the wisdom of Pitt's policy. Bostonians rejoiced in the successes of the empire and paid scant attention to the economic costs involved.

In the midst of celebrating victories in Canada, Bostonians learned that they were to lose Pownall. In the world of the eighteenth-century British empire, the governorship of Massachusetts had never been a particularly juicy plum, and so Pownall accepted a more lucrative post as governor of South Carolina. On 3 June 1760 Pownall rode from the State House down King Street to embark at Long Wharf. It was an elegant scene and a tribute to His Excellency as "both Houses attended him in a body to his barge, and took leave of him in terms as complimentary to his talents as they were creditable to themselves."

Two months after Pownall's departure, Sir Francis Bernard, formerly governor of New Jersey, arrived in Boston as the newly commissioned royal governor. From the moment he stepped from his barge, Bernard felt a chill wind from the shore. Rumors were about that Bernard had come to Massachusetts unwillingly and had asked His Majesty for a more profitable post in a warmer clime. His request had been refused. Under the best of circumstances, Bernard would have found Pownall a difficult act to follow. Circumstances, however, were not at their best, and they would soon grow worse. In later years, as an older generation of revolutionaries looked back on Bernard's arrival, they saw a turning point, a moment when history veered onto a different path, one in this case that would lead to revolution. Events did indeed begin to take on an ominous cast once Bernard took office. Samuel Adams had once remarked that "a governor's station is very slippery." The new governor was skating on thin ice.

On 11 September 1760 Judge Stephen Sewall, chief justice of the province, died. During his tenure Thomas Pownall had, in an agreeable moment, promised James Otis, Sr., a distinguished lawyer from Barnstable County, the chief justice position once it became available. But now with Pownall gone the decision was Bernard's, and the new governor determined to turn it to his advantage.

Bernard found the province and the town factious. There were men in both the General Court and the town meeting who held ideas about rights and liberties that were, in the eyes of the new governor, positively "unconstitutional." Rather than face such men directly, Bernard plotted a more subtle strategy based on "management and intrigue." The governor was arrogant and pompous, and thought he was dealing with a cast of provincial buffoons. He was wrong.

Bernard's first "intrigue" centered on the newly vacant post. Rewarding Otis offered Bernard nothing except the dubious honor of fulfilling another man's promise. Otis was too independent and his son James, also a lawyer, was too unpredictable. For chief justice Bernard needed someone whose Tory sympathies were beyond reproach and who might draw into provincial government others with similar inclinations. Thomas Hutchinson was his man.

Hutchinson's credentials were impeccable. His family roots were as deep in the province as those of the Adams family. His great-great-grandmother was Anne Hutchinson, protagonist of the antinomian controversy, the woman who had rocked the colony by challenging clerical authority. Born in Boston in 1711, Thomas had graduated from Harvard with the class of 1727. In 1734 he married Margaret Sanford, daughter of the governor of Rhode Island. Margaret's sister married Andrew Oliver, thus joining together two of the most powerful families in the province, the Hutchinsons and the Olivers. When Hutchinson's father died in 1739 Thomas inherited most of the very considerable family estate.

As a conservative merchant, Hutchinson had been instrumental in slaying the land bank and boasted of his role in bringing that "wicked Mony to an End." He was appointed justice of the peace and judge of probate by both Governors Shirley and Pownall and had also served on a variety of special commissions. He was elected to the council in 1749, and in 1758 he became lieutenant governor. Thomas Hutchinson was wealthy, well connected, conservative, and reliable, all important credentials, in Bernard's opinion at least, for appointment to the province's highest judicial post. That Hutchinson had no legal training and his only experience with the law had been as a judge of probate, a fairly perfunctory calling, did not concern the new governor. However, the appointee's lack of legal qualifications did not escape notice of members of the Boston bar. Young John Adams, only recently admitted to the bar and full of professional pride, fumed that Hutchinson, a man bred to "husbandry, merchandise [and] politics," could never master the law. He was, according to Adams, thoroughly unfit for the bench and seating him would constitute a slap at the law.

As chief justice, Hutchinson would preside over the highest and most important court in the province. Under his predecessors, the court had become an important machine in the enforcement of the various laws regulating trade. For Boston merchants, many of whom made their living by violating the laws of trade, who sat on the court was a matter of interest. Others not directly involved in clandestine smuggling, like Adams, had had their suspicions aroused as well, for they had always viewed the court as a symbol of royal prerogative, a prerogative they feared Hutchinson would broaden.

Bernard truly believed that Hutchinson was a brilliant choice and that the people of the province would agree with him. In holding that notion, the new governor showed how out of touch he was with those he had been sent to govern.

Hutchinson's appointment provoked ire not only from those who opposed him on political grounds but from other quarters as well. Among the latter group were those who viewed the lieutenant governor, and his relations the Olivers, as plundering pluralists determined to garner every profitable governmental position. That charge struck home, for between them the Hutchinson and Oliver clans held a raft of key posts. Pluralism was not uncommon in the eighteenth century, but even by the standards of the time, the Hutchinsons and Olivers pushed the limits of tolerance.

Pluralism, politics, and economics alone would have been sufficient to raise a storm over Hutchinson, but spicing these aggravations was the injured pride of James "Jemmy" Otis. Violently emotional, irascible, and brilliant, Jemmy Otis may well have been mad in 1760. Mad or not, however, he was a skilled lawyer and orator.

When news of Hutchinson's appointment reached Barnstable, young Otis, at least according to Bernard, swore that he would avenge the insult to his father and "set the whole province in a flame, though he perished in the attempt." With that oath, he rode to Boston to carry out his threat. Not long after arriving in town, Jemmy Otis got his chance to wreak vengeance.

CHAPTER 4

The Battle Begins

❖
❖

On 25 October 1760 His Majesty George II died, succeeded by his grandson George III. In Boston the usual public lamentations spilled forth, minute guns echoed from Castle William, bells tolled their doleful respects, but in point of fact, the king had never been popular in the town. He was vulgar, cantankerous, dissolute, and German. His final departure took place fittingly enough, not in the royal bedchamber, surrounded by loving relations, but in "a water-closet at Kensington."

According to law, at the demise of the monarch, the writs issued in his name expired. New writs would need to be issued. For customs officers in Massachusetts, the requirement to seek new writs could not have come at a more inconvenient time.

Among the most valuable weapons a customs officer held in his arsenal were writs of assistance. These writs granted officers wide discretion in ferreting out illegal goods. Under the old administration of Boston's amiable collector Benjamin Barrons, the latitude offered by the writs had caused little worry. Everyone knew that Barrons found merchants' bribes a surer way to wealth than the king's shillings. With Barons as collector and Pownall as governor, the smuggling merchants of Boston felt secure. To their consternation Barrons was relieved of his post in December 1759. Bernard replaced Pownall soon thereafter.

Since the royal governor took one-third of the proceeds from seized goods, Bernard had more than a passing interest in strictly enforcing the laws. Barron's dismissal, Bernard's cupidity, and the expiring writs together produced a crisis in Boston when James Cockle, collector at Salem, asked the province's superior court to issue him a writ. Uncertain about its jurisdiction, the court deferred issuance and decided to hold a hearing. Chief Justice Jonathan Sewall set a date in February 1761. By that date, though, Sewall was dead, and Thomas Hutchinson had assumed his seat.

Like most of his fellow Bostonians, Samuel Adams paid keen attention to the drama unfolding in the court's State House chamber. There was a hint of pleasure in his aspect, for the question of the writs promised to drive splinters among the merchants, men whose actions had brought him grief in the past. On one hand were the smuggling merchants, who loathed the writs nearly as much as they despised Bernard, and a good number of whom were members of the loosely knit Boston Society for Encouraging Trade and Commerce. At the other end of the spectrum were merchants, Hutchinson and his kin for example, whose ties bound them to the royal governor.

Determined to thwart any reissuance of the writs, the merchants engaged James Otis to argue their case. Otis was brilliant. Addressing the stern-faced, scarlet-robed justices, Otis was explosive in his delivery. He declared that he spoke for the "inhabitants of Boston," that he intended to defend "British liberties." Lest any suspect his motives, he announced that he would accept no fee for his services, a nice contrast to Bernard's well-known avarice and Hutchinson's grasping.

There in the superior court chamber, perhaps for the first time, at least in Boston, citizens heard principles proclaimed that were to be revolutionary in their consequences. Adams and his fellow townsmen nodded in agreement as Otis described the writs as the "worst instrument of arbitrary power, the most destructive to English liberty, and the fundamental principles of the constitution." In rising decibels, Otis charged that the writs were "the zenith of arbitrary power." According to the Barnstable firebrand, the court should "demolish this monster of oppression, and tear into rags this remnant of Star chamber Tyranny." Otis's argument began in the bedrock of the law and then rushed across the legal frontier into the nebulous world of "Natural Law" and "Rights." He announced that it mattered not if Parliament had enacted the writs, for they ran "against the fundamental principles of law." What did that mean? Was Otis referring to some greater and higher power than king and Parliament? Here was a truly romantic notion, not subject to proof, but wide open for interpretation, particularly by a community whose deep-seated beliefs about its origin, history, and rights differed substantially from prevailing views in the mother country. For Hutchinson, whose mind was strictly bounded by the text of law, Otis's arguments were echoes in an empty barrel.

They were not, however, lost on others. Otis's performance made him a hero. Samuel Adams certainly thought so and so too did his cousin John, just beginning his legal practice in Boston. More than a half century later, and with a certain degree of embellishment, Adams the lawyer restaged the tableau:

> [N]ear the fire were seated five judges, with Lieutenant Governor Hutchinson at their head as chief justice, all in their new fresh robes of scarlet English cloth, in their broad bands, and immense judicial wigs [and against them James Otis] a flame of fire! With the promptitude of classical allusions, a depth of research, a profusion of legal authorities, a prophetic glare of his eyes into futurity, and a rapid torrent of impetuous eloquence, he hurried away all before him. Every man of an [immense] crowded audience appeared to me to go away, as I did, ready to take up arms against writs of assistance. Then and there the child independence was born.

To no one's surprise, certainly not James Otis's, the court eventually upheld the issuance of the writs. Even before their ef-

fects could be felt, however, other, more significant consequences of the hearing emerged. This case had thrown a sizable number of Boston merchants into common cause with
Samuel Adams and the town meeting caucus. It was a fragile
alliance, but whatever their differences the town's activists
and its merchants now had a common foe. It was that faction
or party associated with the governor and the court party, increasingly symbolized in the person of Thomas Hutchinson.

News of Otis's argument wafted inland. When a contribu-
tor to the *Boston Gazette* wrote that Otis's arguments were
"conclusive," many in the countryside agreed. In politically
active towns throughout the province, groups, much like the
caucus in Boston, had gathered to stand in opposition to the
royal governor. Never orderly or linear, the evolution of opposition had been idiosyncratic and opportunistic. It had also
been independent: The country towns always suspicious of
Boston, and Bostonians, always suspicious of the country
towns, had certainly not set out to be allies. The writs, however, had made them so. It was not an equal partnership, of
course, for the principal leaders were Bostonians, among
whom Otis, although Cape Cod born, was now counted. The
Boston caucus, people in the country towns, and merchants
were joined, and for the moment at least Otis stood at their
head. How long and in what form they might remain together
was another question entirely.

Samuel Adams admired Otis's brazenness and envied his
skills at oratory. While clever with a pen, Adams had a hesi-
tant speaking manner that prevented him from delivering the
kind of stem-winders Otis reeled off. For the time being, however, Adams, struggling to earn a living and raise two children, was content to march behind Otis as he carried the ban-
ner of the town.

In a small way, though, Adams found an opportunity to
snipe at the opposition. Like his fellow churchmen, he feared
that the Anglicans were conspiring to send a bishop to America, and he saw a sinister aim in their every effort to strengthen
their church in America. The recent increase in Anglican mis-

sions to the Indians was a special worry. David Brainerd was still Adams's hero, and the thought that Anglican missionaries were spreading error where Brainerd had brought truth was distressing as was the likelihood that the secular power of the Church of England would also thereby be enhanced. For reasons of faith and politics, in January 1762 Adams joined with several others, including James Otis and John Hancock, to form a society to promote Congregational missions to the Indians. While the proselytizing of neither the Anglicans nor the Congregationalists bore much fruit, the latter at least had the satisfaction of seeing the former fail.

In quick succession, Otis was elected town moderator and representative to the General Court. In the court he allied with his father, James Senior, who was not only representative from Barnstable but speaker as well. The brace of Otises did all in their power to challenge Bernard and cause difficulty for his administration. They even managed to reduce the salary of the person they most particularly disliked, Chief Justice Thomas Hutchinson, from £750 to £700.

Yet while Otis, Adams, and others delighted in their small victories, elsewhere larger issues were being debated, issues that would eventually decide the fate of the empire. In 1763, after more than seven years of war, representatives of England and France met at Paris to fashion a peace. British arms had been triumphant and so to the English went the greater share of the spoils. The booty was considerable. France ceded all claim to Acadia, Cape Breton, Canada, and the islands of the St. Lawrence, retaining some fishing rights on the Newfoundland banks and possession of the islands of St. Pierre and Miquelon. France also gave over to Great Britain all her territory east of the Mississippi. In return, Great Britain agreed to restore to France the West Indian islands of Guadeloupe and Martinique.

That the government took Canada and not the sugar islands seemed a mystery to many. After all, Canada had never been particularly profitable for France and promised little more for England. The ministry, however, was less concerned about immediate profit and more focused on strategic aims.

They were imperialists who envisioned the empire as a spacious and prosperous enterprise governed from London. Throughout the war, government officials in London had come to know and resent how independent the American colonies could be. The need for colonial cooperation, even when it was in short supply however, forced London officials grudgingly to overlook instances of ill behavior from their American cousins. Were Canada to remain French, the colonials would keep their lever, for as long as a powerful enemy sat to the north, London would always have to be wary of alienating the colonials. In a curious way, the French presence in Canada kept Britain dependent on the colonies. If imperial reform were to be realized, with power shifting to London and away from the colonies, this dependency would have to be eliminated. Prescient British officials, knew that securing Canada would give them a freer hand in dealing with the mainland colonies.

Boston welcomed news of the Treaty of Paris. Having lived under the threat of what Cotton Mather once referred to as "half Frenchified Indians and half Indianized French" for more than a century, the people of Boston rejoiced that they had been delivered from their enemies. Little did they understand that they would now be delivered up to the empire.

Faced with a huge war debt (£140 million) the ministry was determined to "reform" the empire in a manner that would allow them to extract revenue from the colonies. There were only two means to accomplish that end: Either the colonies would of their own accord furnish funds or Parliament had to seize them. The first course was highly unlikely and the latter was troublesome. If Parliament intended to draw money from the colonies, it would mean intruding into local affairs in unprecedented ways. Like the townspeople of nearby Sudbury, who more than a century earlier had told the colony leaders that they would be governed only by men of their own choosing, the citizens of Boston were ready to assert their autonomy. Indeed, strong local government had always been the wrench in the mercantilist system. For Parliament to make the system work efficiently now would mean invading that which Bostonians held most sacred—autonomy.

From the distant frontier came one of the first signs of parliamentary vigor. On 7 October the king signed the Proclamation of 1763. Having endured endless problems centering on Indian-white relations, the ministry decided that the best preventive measure was segregation; hence the proclamation stipulated there would be, for a time at least, no further settlement west of the Appalachians. While settlers and land speculators hollered in protest, Bostonians hardly blinked. After all, their interests were not involved. Within a few months, though, their isolationism would be challenged.

In the spring of 1764 Boston was ill prepared for more bad news. The town still had numerous empty lots where homes and shops destroyed in the fire of 1760 had yet to be rebuilt. Nearly 25 percent of the town's male population had been taken up for service in the war; 10 percent of those never returned, leaving behind a considerable number of widows and orphans to be supported at the public charge. High taxes were levied, but less than half were collected.

No one understood the town's poverty better than its newly elected tax collector, Samuel Adams. There could hardly have been a worse time to be saddled with a job that was never particularly rewarding, financially or otherwise. That Adams accepted election is a measure of his desperate need for income. Many wealthy Bostonians had left the town to escape smallpox and taxes. (Adams's own children Samuel and Hannah were inoculated in March 1764 and survived.) Adams had no means to track down and collar these tax cheats, yet by province law he was personally responsible for their taxes, a debt that could be charged against his estate. In fact, the law was rarely enforced, and only Adams's enemies gave serious thought to punishing him for not accomplishing the impossible. In later years, as revolutionary fever climbed, Adams was pilloried by his Tory foes for his failure to collect taxes and often accused of having used his post to favor his friends.

Despite his limitations as a tax collector, Adams could not have picked a more propitious occasion for his public debut. For more than twenty years he had been active in town politics, but thus far he had been content to remain out of office. The salary was clearly a lure, but Adams must have been energized by events around him—the writs of assistance, the Treaty of Paris, rising partisanship in the town. The future was uncertain, but it could not help but be interesting. Adams was not one to sit idly by.

In London George Grenville, chancellor of the exchequer and Pitt's brother-in-law, had a plan. Like Pitt he sought to strengthen the empire by oiling the gears of mercantilism. According to his reckoning, shared by many others, the empire was losing a tidy fortune in both trade and taxes under the policy of "salutary neglect." Looking at a debt of £140 million, its interest running to £5 million a year, all to be supported by a paltry annual income of £8 million, Grenville hungered to revitalize orthodox mercantilism, a system that promised a robust income. The Revenue Act of 1764, better known as the Sugar Act, was his first step.

In May 1763 Grenville studied a report on the state of customs collection in America. It was shocking how little revenue, barely £1800, had been collected. It was even more shocking that to collect that £1800 the government had spent £7500. The customs service was losing money, lots of it! In its conclusion the report alluded to the Americans' considerable success with smuggling and made several recommendations for tightening up enforcement.

With dispatch, Grenville moved on the administrative front. Customs officers, many of whom lived in England and left the day-to-day operations to colonial functionaries, were ordered to their posts. At the same time governors were instructed to keep a watch on customs officials and to report any lapses in the performance of their duty. Grenville also succeeded in persuading the Royal Navy to patrol coastal waters and pounce on smugglers.

The report that helped move Grenville to action also suggested a revision in the duty on molasses. Ever since the Act of 1733, the duty had been assessed at the rate of 6 pence per gallon. But molasses was selling at only 12 pence per gallon, and so the duty was grossly prohibitive and was rarely paid. The report recommended reducing the duty to 3 pence per gallon.

Even at 3 pence, the duty, if collected, would do great harm to the West Indian trade, one of the mainstays of Boston's economy. Already reeling under the woeful effects of the war, the West Indian trade might well collapse should this duty be collected.

"Trade is a nice and delicate lady; she must be courted and won by soft addresses. She will not bear the rude hand of a ravisher." Such were the romantic sentiments of one Boston writer. Others less seduced by metaphors were more worried about the rights of Bostonians being assailed. Both Samuel Adams and James Otis saw the Sugar Act for what it really was—the opening round of a new policy designed to raise an American revenue and restrict American rights. Adams was the first to respond.

As was the custom, at the spring meeting the town chose representatives to the General Court. Elected were Royall Tyler, James Otis, Thomas Cushing, and Oxenbridge Thacher. Also according to tradition, the meeting provided the representatives with instructions. In light of recent developments, the instructions of 24 May 1764 took on particular import, and Samuel Adams was entrusted with the task of writing them. After reciting a litany of reasons why Parliament's new acts were unwise, Adams drove to the heart of the matter:

> But what still heightens our apprehensions is, that these unexpected Proceedings may be preparatory to new Taxations upon us: For if our Trade may be taxed why not our Lands? Why not the Produce of our Lands and everything we possess or make use of? This we apprehend annihilates our Charter Right to govern and tax ourselves—It strikes at our British Privileges, which as we have never forfeited

them, we hold in common with our Fellow Subjects who are Natives of Britain: If Taxes are laid upon us in any shape without our having a legal Representation where they are laid, are we not reduced from the Character of free Subjects to the miserable State of tributary Slaves?

Just weeks after Adams had delivered his instructions, Otis issued *The Rights of the British Colonies Asserted and Proved.* He argued that civil government was given by God to all free men who then had the right to "devolve" that power onto a representative government. They did not, Otis argued, surrender power, but only delegated it to their representatives. In the English system this power rested with "King, lords and commons." The colonies were an integral part of this system. Distance did not diminish rights.

Otis celebrated the English tradition. He called it "the most free one, and by far the best, now existing on earth." By it "every man in the dominions is a free man." He noted that in this system no man could be taxed except by his consent given through his representatives. This was the heart of the matter, for Otis then suggested that there were those in England who sought to subvert and deny this right to the colonies. This was unacceptable and in contradiction to the traditions of English constitutional government. No part of the empire ought to be taxed without its consent, and thus, all colonies were entitled to representation in the supreme legislative body. Otis was in line with his reading of history. Yet implicit in his argument was a willingness to accept an inferior position for the colonial assembly. He believed that Parliament was supreme in all matters. Samuel Adams and James Otis, it would soon become clear, viewed history through different prisms.

Otis's understanding of history was static and rigid. It lacked the flexibility to accommodate the nuances of 150 years of colonial development. It said nothing about the rise of representative government throughout the colonies and sadly misunderstood its evolution in Massachusetts and Boston in particular. The "quest for power" on the part of local government had been a constant theme throughout the colonies, and while the results were mixed, no where was government in the mainland colonies the same in 1764 as it was at the time of founding.

Otis's perspective on the present as well as the past was anglocentric. He viewed the early settlers as transplanted Englishmen and women who, driven by a medley of motives, set sail for Massachusetts.

Along with their baggage they carried with them all the rights of Englishmen. They also brought over obligations, chief among them recognition of the supremacy of Parliament. In Otis's mind, local government was a mere convenience, a simple means of addressing local needs and enforcing the will of the legitimate authority in London. Otis did not challenge the absolute sovereignty of Parliament; instead, he questioned whether it was using its power wisely. The colonists of his time, just like the first settlers, were perfectly content to rely on English institutions as long as those institutions did not violate their fundamental rights as citizens of the empire.

Despite his admiration for Otis, Adams did not share his historical perspective. Whereas Otis saw unity of purpose, Adams saw variety. He agreed that the first settlers were in heart and soul transplanted Englishmen, but he also argued that they were something else in addition. They had not been passive for 150 years; rather, they had been vigorously active in shaping their own destiny. The people of Massachusetts Bay had covenanted together to form both churches and governments, and over time both institutions had grown in power, influence, and independence. By no means was Adams ready to assert that Parliament lacked authority in the province, but history was nudging him toward that conclusion.

Otis, the lawyer, looked to the law to discern the relationship among king, Parliament, and colonies. Adams, the politician, looked to history, as he interpreted it, for his justifications. On the other side of the Atlantic, Edmund Burke, one of the parliamentary leaders opposing the king, also saw the problem of the widening gulf between the colonies and king. Indeed, Parliament would have done well to mind his words when this highly distinguished member reminded his colleagues that when subjects begin to feel the necessity of defining their rights, it should be taken as "a sure symptom of an ill-conducted state." Instead, authorities in London, confident that their power was unassailable, smiled at the lack of focus and unity in the colonies.

Of all the ports in America, Boston was by far the one most deeply involved in the West India trade. Her wails of protest over the Sugar Act were far more shrill than the muted noises rising up from New York and Philadelphia. That Boston suffered so much, and the other ports so little, played into Grenville's hands. Try as they might, Boston merchants simply could not rally support among the other colonies. The aggrieved merchants sent their own petitions to London, but they were ineffectual. Even Otis's complaint that the colonies were not represented in Parliament was casually dismissed with the reminder that most Englishmen, not able to meet property qualifications or living in boroughs without an MP, were not directly represented in Parliament. Thomas Whately, one of Grenville's political henchmen, struck a common chord when he asserted these Englishmen along with the colonists were *virtually* represented. This is to say that once an MP took his seat he represented not the constituency that had sent him but rather all subjects of the king. That argument made no sense to Bostonians, who were accustomed to knowing, electing, instructing, and hectoring their representatives in the most direct way possible.

Grenville would have been well advised to heed his success with the Sugar Act. No one had denied Parliament could levy duties. Moreover, enacting measures that struck selectively at particular colonies prevented discontent from spreading. Grenville strayed from these principles—historical justification and well-reasoned political strategy—when he crafted the Stamp Act.

Despite his growing involvement in politics, Samuel Adams found time to fall in love. By the end of 1764, he had been a widower for more than seven years. It could not have been easy keeping house and raising children alone. The object of his reawakened affections was Elizabeth Wells. She was 13 years younger, unmarried, and the daughter of Francis Wells, an Englishman who had settled in the town in 1723. Family records describe Francis Wells as a merchant, but he referred to himself as a distiller.

Elizabeth and Samuel were married on 6 December 1764 by Samuel's first father-in-law, Samuel Checkley. One of 12 children with a large extended family, Elizabeth brought her husband a considerable number of ready-made allies. On the other hand, the size of the Wells family also meant that Elizabeth probably brought little or no dowry to the match. The marriage left the Samuel Adamses as poorly off as they had ever been.

Poverty was, though, part of the Adams image. It may have been a carefully cultivated trait. In contrast to the great Tories—Hutchinson, the Olivers et al., and even some "patriot" leaders such as Hancock, Warren, and Otis—Samuel Adams dressed and played the part of an ordinary Bostonian. He may not have been as "rumpled" as some observers believed, but even in the famous Copley portrait of 1774, in which he points dramatically to the Massachusetts charter, he is dressed in a remarkably common fashion. When compared to Copley's other portraits of famous Bostonians, especially his renowned rendering of an elegant John Hancock attired in fine purple with gold trim, Samuel Adams came across as a man of the people. At the same time, with the precious charter at his fingertips, Copley left no room to doubt Adams's political attachments.

Adams's wife also helped cultivate the simple image. Elizabeth Wells Adams was a good, solid New England wife, nearly as plump as Samuel himself. Reputed to be the best housekeeper in Boston, she certainly had more direct contact with the daily chores of life than Dorothy Quincy Hancock or Ruth Cunningham Otis.

Along with genteel poverty Adams also crafted an image of piety. He regularly attended services at the Old South, just up the street from his home. To his enemies, particularly Thomas Hutchinson, he was a Pharisee who used religion as a "stalking horse" behind which he masked his evil machinations. More likely he was a conventional Congregationalist who for the most part held to the forms of that religion and shared its beliefs. By family tradition, he loved to sing and was known to have "an exquisite ear for music, and a charming voice." Early in 1765, not long after his marriage, that "charming voice" was raised to new heights of protest over the Stamp Act.

CHAPTER 5

Sons of Liberty

❖
❖

Boston was a gloomy place in winter. Gray skies, white ground, and blustery winds kept citizens at home and ships in port. On 9 January 1765, however, hibernation was interrupted as the General Court assembled for its winter session. Around town, small knots of men gathered at taverns and coffeehouses where their conversations centered on the baneful effects of the Sugar Act as well as fresh, even more distressing rumors from London. Foreboding grew almost unbearable when a financial earthquake shook the town.

During the years of conflict with France, some merchants of the town engaged heavily in war contracting. No one had been more deeply involved than Nathaniel Wheelwright, whose rampant speculations indebted him to nearly every trader in Boston and many in London. Peace broke his bubble and on 16 January he suspended payment on his obligations.

Wheelwright might have survived the trauma of peace if his creditors had been able to sustain some hope for the future. Because the Sugar Act made it look so bleak, however, those holding his paper felt compelled to collect. As is so often the case in matters of financial faith, the pack closed in all at once. Wheelwright's woes spilled over onto others, and like shallow-rooted willows, a succession of Boston merchants tumbled into bankruptcy. Otis saw it as a catastrophe and described the effect on the town "such was the Consternation for some little time that people appeared with pale Horror and Dread, and when a little recovered run about the City. Widows and Orphans that are ruined can only bewail their fate, the more resolute have been pulling and hauling, attaching and summoning to secure themselves, but it was too late to shut the Stable door."

Grenville had little understanding and no real sympathy for the townspeople of Boston. Nothing would divert him from his determination to raise a revenue in America. He believed Parliament had every right to tax the colonies, and he intended to do just that. Indeed, embedded in the parliamentary debates over the Sugar Act were several references to an impending Stamp Act. Suspecting that Americans would not react well to such a tax, Grenville attempted to dull the edge of opposition by delaying passage for a year. He did so, he said, so that the colonies might have an opportunity to propose their own scheme for raising an American revenue. Jasper Mauduit, the agent of Massachusetts, reported to the General Court that "The Stamp duty you will see, is deferr'd till next Year. I mean the actual laying it: Mr. Grenville being willing to give to the Provinces their option to raise that or some equivalent tax, Desirous as he express'd himself to consult the Ease, the Quiet, and the Goodwill of the Colonies."

At best, George Grenville was disingenuous. His invitation to the colonies, never sent officially but always communicated informally, was vague. How much revenue was needed? How should the burden be apportioned among the colonies? To what purpose would it be applied? Grenville offered no answers, not to Parliament, his own ministers, or the governors. He intended to levy a Stamp Tax. The rest was subterfuge.

During the debates over the Sugar Act, some politicians, both in London and America, including William Pitt and Benjamin Franklin, had made a distinction between an internal and an external tax. External taxes, those that regulated trade and were not directly assigned and collected from citizens, were, they argued, traditionally acceptable, whereas internal taxes had never been levied and were not constitutional. The point was fatuous. Either Parliament was supreme and could legislate in all matters, as Grenville maintained, or it was not. Whatever others might believe, parliamentary sovereignty, in the opinion of George Grenville, was not partible.

On 6 February the matter came to a head in Parliament. Charles Townshend, no friend to the colonies, rose to speak in support of the Stamp Act. He asked rhetorically, "And now will these Americans, Children planted by our Care, nourished up by our Opulence, and protected by our Arms, will they grudge to contribute their mite to relieve us from the heavy weight of that burden which we lie under." Townshend's view of the colonies as protected children "nourished" by a kind imperial mother troubled Adams, particularly in light of London's most recent request for a sign of their appreciation, the Sugar Act.

Townshend's remarks did not go unchallenged. Isaac Barre, a leading English Whig and one of Adams's heroes, delivered a fiery retort. His response so electrified Boston that, at Adams's suggestion, town meeting agreed to hang his portrait in Faneuil Hall. Adams uttered amen to Barre's view of history. "They planted by your Care?" bellowed Barre. "No! your Oppressions planted them in America. They fled from your Tyranny to a then uncultivated and inhospitable Country— where they exposed themselves to almost all the hardships to which human Nature is liable. They met all these hardships with pleasure, compared with those they suffered in their own Country, from the hands of those who should have been their Friends." In his spirited attack on the ministry's policies Barre went on to recount the history of the relationship between colonies and mother country. Members of Parliament were visibly angered by Barre's attacks.

> They nourished by *your* indulgence? they grew by your neglect of them: as soon as you began to care about them, that Care was Exercised in sending persons to rule over them, in one Department and another, who were perhaps the

Deputies of Deputies to some Member of this house—sent to Spy out their Lyberty, to misrepresent their Actions and to prey upon Em; men whose behaviour on many Occasions has caused the Blood of those Sons of Liberty to recoil within them; men promoted to the highest Seats of Justice, some, who to my knowledge were glad by going to a foreign Country to Escape being brought to the Bar of a Court of Justice in their own.

They protected by *your* Arms? they have nobly taken up Arms in your defence, have Exerted a Valour amidst their constant and Laborious industry for the defence of a Country, whose frontier, while drench'd in blood, its interior Parts have yielded all its little Savings to your Emolument. And believe me, remember I this Day told you so, that same Spirit of freedom which actuated that people at first, will accompany them still.—But prudence forbids me to explain myself further.

Barre's appeal notwithstanding, on its third reading the bill passed by a margin of 205 to 49. On 22 March the king affixed his seal.

Late in April, copies of the act, and news of the debate surrounding it, arrived in Boston. For weeks, Adams had heard rumors and reports; still, he was shocked. Stamps purchased from official distributors were to be attached to legal documents, college diplomas, newspapers, licenses, pamphlets, playing cards, dice, and almanacs. There was hardly a segment of society not affected by the measure.

On 1 November the act was to go into effect. In the intervening months stamps were to be printed and prepared for distribution. On the assumption that local citizens would have less trouble selling stamps than placemen (political appointees) from London, Grenville decided to appoint them as distributors. He would soon discover the seriousness of his miscalculation.

Andrew Oliver, Thomas Hutchinson's brother-in-law, became the most unfortunate man in Boston when he was appointed stamp distributor. Even though his commission had yet to arrive, neither had the stamps for that matter, and by early summer it was public knowledge that the post was his. He was even building a new brick office on Kilby Street, reportedly the place from which he would conduct the stamp business.

At first Boston was slow to respond. Still caught in the web of failures spinning out from Wheelwright's bankruptcy, and mired in a general stagnation of trade brought on by the Sugar Act and a postwar slump, townsmen failed to anticipate the impact of the new act. In June, Otis roused the General Court from its slumber with a proposal for a general congress of the colonies. On 8 June the House approved a circular letter to be sent to all the other colonies inviting them to convene at New York in October "to consider of a general and united, dutiful, loyal and humble Representation of their Condition to His Majesty and the Parliament; and to implore relief." Three men were elected to represent Massachusetts: James Otis, Timothy Ruggles, and Oliver Partridge. Of the three only Otis could be deemed a member sympathetic to the opposition. Ruggles and Partridge were friends of the government; indeed, Bernard had boasted to his superiors in London that it was through his politicking that Ruggles and Partridge were selected. They were, according to his Excellency, "prudent and discreet men such as I am assured will never consent to any undutiful or improper application to the Government of Great Britain." Bernard's conceit was well founded, for not only were Ruggles and Partridge safe, but so too, for the moment at least, was James Otis.

Otis was irascible, unpredictable, and insane. Believing as he did in the sovereignty of Parliament, Otis was struggling with the ever more popular notion of American rights. He oscillated between those poles, but London's attractive power proved the more intense. Shortly before he rode off to New York Otis was reported to have said, "If the government at home don't very soon send forces to keep the peace of this province they will be cutting one anothers throats from one End, to the other of it."

Otis's statement left his friends wondering. It also sent them looking for new leadership. On 9 July Oxenbridge

Thacher died, which left a vacancy in the Boston delegation to the General Court. Almost immediately a ground swell arose in favor of Samuel Adams's election to the vacant seat.

With prospects for his election bright, Adams took the opportunity during the summer to distance himself from Otis. While he held high regard for Otis, he did not share his friend's increasingly conservative views; and by the election, Boston voters suggested that neither did they. In May the Virginia House of Burgesses gave Adams an opportunity to distance himself from Otis and claim leadership of the popular faction.

Having nearly completed the business of their spring session by the end of May, the members of Burgesses were winding down their agenda. Many members had already left for home when news of the Stamp Act arrived in Williamsburg. On the afternoon of 30 May, Patrick Henry, a newly elected delegate from Hanover County, rose to speak in protest. Precisely what Henry said was uncertain; what really mattered was what was reported and believed. The story that made its way to Boston and electrified the town was that Henry stood in Burgesses and proclaimed, "Caesar had his Brutus; Charles the First his Cromwell; and George the Third may profit by their example. If this be treason, make the most of it."

Henry and his allies did "make the most of it." With little opposition, they pushed through the chamber a series of resolves. The official records of Burgesses are a bit murky on the number of resolves, and on how many of that floating number were actually approved, but again perception was as good as reality for the colonists who did fear an all-powerful monarchy. Throughout the colonies the Virginia Resolves were printed as seven in number.

Henry's resolves declared that Parliament had no right to tax the colonies and the people of Virginia were not bound to yield obedience to any laws of Parliament intended to levy taxes. Should there be any in the colony with a contrary view the final resolve thundered, "That any Person who by Speaking or Writing, assert or maintain, That any Persons, other than the General Assembly of this Colony, have any Right or

Authority to impose any Tax whatever on the Inhabitants shall be Deemed, An ENEMY TO THIS HIS MAJESTY'S COLONY."

Adams could barely contain his joy as he read Henry's resolves. Boston stood in shame that the Old Dominion had been so firm and first in line to defend American rights. He was determined to overtake his colleagues in Virginia. In this he was assisted by a series of events erupting in the summer of 1765.

Like most urban areas in the eighteenth century, Boston had mobs, roving gangs of men defiant of authority and often violent, whose passions were often ignited by some act of government. In Boston these were sailors, ropewalkers, teamsters, dockworkers, men who were itinerant, casual, unskilled tavern denizens, the flotsam and jetsam of seaports, always available for street scenes, and, since the Sugar Act, more available and more on the streets than ever. Suspicious of authority, and often mistreated, mobs could be tools in the hands of politicians. They were useful at embarrassing and intimidating officials.

For generations Bostonians had celebrated Guy Fawkes Day by a procession through town of two effigies of the pope, one paraded by a gang from the North End and another by a similar set of ruffians from the South End. By the early 1760s the South Enders were led by the renowned Ebenezer MacIntosh, Boston's best known cordwainer. As the two bands marched their rounds, lathered up in rum and gin, they eventually ran into each other. It was always a Donnybrook, with fists, clubs, and rocks producing a number of injuries. In November 1764 the riots had turned particularly ugly. Amid the melee, a young boy had been run over by a cart and killed. MacIntosh was arrested and charged with disturbing the peace. He easily secured an acquittal from a local jury and left court more famous than before, now dubbed "Captain MacIntosh," commander of the South End.

If Captain MacIntosh could supply the cast of characters, others in the town could supply organization and purpose that went beyond mere anti-Catholic hysteria. Early in the summer emerged a shadowy assemblage of nine men who would ever after be referred to as the "Loyal Nine." None were lowborn, but neither were they highborn. They perched midway on Boston's social ladder; they were able to reach up or climb down. Best known among the company was Benjamin Edes, publisher of the *Boston Gazette*. Noticeably absent was Samuel Adams. His association with these gentlemen was close enough, however, that he could well have been considered a shadowy tenth member of the Loyal Nine.

Thanks to Grenville's clumsiness, the Loyal Nine had no difficulty identifying a proper target for the mayhem they set out to orchestrate about the Stamp Act. Their choice became apparent to all on the morning of 14 August. Hanging from a tree on Newbury Street near Boston Neck was an effigy of Andrew Oliver. A particularly nice touch, swinging next to Oliver, was a large boot out of which crawled the devil. Lord Bute was one of the king's most unpopular ministers. The pun was just too delicious for MacIntosh to resist giving it his personal mark. For weeks, Edes's *Gazette* had been enflaming the town against Oliver and Grenville's stamps, while the Loyal Nine and MacIntosh had been out agitating their own constituencies. That Oliver's effigy should now be dangling from the limb of a tree was hardly a surprise.

Chief Justice Hutchinson ordered the sheriff to cut down his brother-in-law's effigy, but a crowd would not let him near the tree. Bernard summoned the council, whose members, mindful of their personal danger should they act, decided the matter was a petty annoyance best ignored. Insouciance became more studied later in the afternoon when the mob cut down the effigy and paraded it through town and, as they passed directly under the open window of the State House council chamber, they greeted the assembly with three loud huzzas.

From the State House, the mob wended its way down toward the waterfront and Oliver's new office on Kilby Street. Within minutes they had reduced the building to a mere pile of red bricks. Oliver had wisely fled to the safety of Castle William, out in the harbor, where he was joined by Governor Bernard. With Oliver out across the water the crowd moved on to the North End, where they promptly went to work ransacking his elegant home.

Whatever Thomas Hutchinson's faults, he was no coward. While the council quivered and Oliver and Bernard hid behind the walls of Castle William, Hutchinson went into the street in a vain, and perhaps foolhardy, attempt to disperse the crowd. They greeted him with a hail of stones. The next day the mob visited the Hutchinsons. According to his own account they demanded that he "declare to them I had never wrote to England in favor of the Stamp Act." This proud, vain aristocrat refused to answer the summons of the mob. Just as the unruly protesters were ready to rip his house apart, a "grave, elderly tradesman" intervened. Had Adams and company given the slightest command the mob would have surged forward; for the moment, however, the mob was satisfied to withdraw, murmuring threats to return. That same day, Oliver promised to resign as stamp master.

A few days later, Boston's town meeting convened. Adams, MacIntosh, the Loyal Nine, and a host of men who looked as if they had been up late the night before were present in Faneuil Hall. With little discussion they voted to condemn the violence. That was the full extent of the agenda; no action was suggested or taken to bring the mob's leaders to justice or to prevent its reassembling. While he may not have thrown a rock or plucked a brick out of Oliver's building, Samuel Adams was, nonetheless, not unhappy with events. Indeed, remorse was noticeably absent in the town meeting and on the streets of the town.

Having sent the enemy to ground, the mob and the Loyal Nine spent two weeks savoring their victory. They had not forgotten, however, that the Stamp Act was still alive and due to intrude into their lives on 1 November. Additional signs of displeasure would hardly be unexpected.

In the evening hours of 26 August, a group of young boys began to pile wood in front of the Town House. At dark someone lit the bonfire; soon a great crowd was hovering round the flames chanting "Liberty and Property." MacIntosh and his men were at it again. They marched off to the house of Charles Paxton, surveyor and searcher of customs for Boston, a likely target for abuse, particularly by sailors who blamed customs officers for their unemployment. Paxton's landlord met the mob at the door and assured them their quarry had left. They sputtered but were satisfied when the landlord set down drinks for all.

Having finished off a barrel of spirits, the mob decided to hunt other prey, so off they set for the home of William Story, the registrar for the Massachusetts Court of Vice Admiralty. They tore through the door, sacked his house, and carried his official papers to the bonfire, where they were thrown into the blaze. Next, the crowd turned its attention to the biggest game yet—Thomas Hutchinson.

Much has been written about the plundering of Hutchinson's home on this night. The only point of universal agreement is that the mob did its work thoroughly. Whether it did so spontaneously or by design and, if according to plan, whose plan, is a matter open to debate.

Wise conspirators do not keep incriminating records. Samuel Adams was no exception, and there is little in his papers or those of others in Boston, to link him directly to the violence of August 1765. Yet, how could he not have been involved? From beyond its precincts Boston may have appeared unruly, rabble ridden, and lawless. In fact Boston was carefully managed as it had been since the days of Elisha Cooke. It was a tightly formed community (fewer than fifteen thousand people packed into an area of less than a square mile), crisscrossed by kinship lines, with a long tradition of local autonomy and well-directed town meetings. Purposeless violence was not a Boston tradition. What happened in August 1765 was directed, planned, and had, at the very least, the tacit consent of all who knew about it in advance. Adams was among those who knew.

Within hours after the rampage through Hutchinson's home, town meeting convened. Adams was present and, along with his fellow members, he expressed his concern over the violence. As he later wrote to Richard Jackson, however, what was to be expected when Parliament threatened the rights of Americans? Was not the "resentment" of the people justified?

From his sanctuary behind the walls of Castle William, the feckless Bernard wrote a pathetic letter to the king's senior military officer in the colonies, Gen. Thomas Gage, trying to explain why he had failed to keep order in the town. "You are sensible how extremely weak an American Governor is in regard to popular tumults," he whined. To garner support Bernard summoned a meeting of the council.

With the exception of Lieutenant Governor Hutchinson, the Council was as pusillanimous as Bernard. They refused to write Gage to request armed support, probably because they feared for their personal safety should the local mob get wind of the communication. Next they invited Sheriff Greenleaf into their presence to query him about the riot.

Acting on information covertly provided, Greenleaf had arrested MacIntosh. That was the good news. The bad news was that he had also let him go. Soon after MacIntosh was taken into custody, reported the sheriff, "Mr. Nathaniel Coffin, and several other gentlemen, came to him, and told him that it had been agreed that the cadets and many other persons should appear in arms the next evening, as a guard and security against a fresh riot, which was feared, and said to have been threatened, but not a man would appear unless MacIntosh was discharged." As might be expected, Hutchinson was furious; he chastised the sheriff: "You have not done your duty."

As summer faded into fall, tempers in Boston cooled a bit. At Castle William, Bernard fell into a sullen mood. He was deeply bitter toward his superiors in London, particularly Grenville, who had used him badly. He tried to warn them that Bostonians would not abide by the provisions of the Stamp Act. But the authorities had refused to listen, had passed the duty, and told Bernard he must enforce the law. Unhappily, the only force Bernard could apply to enforce the law was summed up in the person of the unfortunate Sheriff Greenleaf.

While Bernard spent his moody days lamenting his circumstance, Samuel Adams and the Sons of Liberty worked to keep the town alert. On 11 September, they gathered on the corner of Essex and Orange Streets beneath the limbs of a large elm tree, the very tree from which they had hung the effigy of Andrew Oliver. It had become a living symbol for the Sons, and now, in a public ceremony followed by the usual drinking and eating, they consecrated the Elm as the "Liberty Tree."

One week later, town meeting assembled for its fall session. First on the agenda was the need to instruct the town's representatives in the General Court. They turned to Adams for help. On 18 September they approved his strongly worded letter to the delegation. Adams set the tone by opening, "At a time when the British American Subjects are every where loudly complaining of arbitrary and unconstitutional Innovations, the Town of Boston cannot any longer remain silent." That statement must have sent a faint chuckle through the crowd. Had Bostonians ever remained "silent"? Adams then went on to rehearse once again his unalterable belief that the Stamp Act was unconstitutional and a violation of the rights of Americans. Adams's star was rising and on the twenty-seventh the voters elected him to replace the deceased Oxenbridge Thacher as a representative in the General Court.

As soon as the House convened, the governor addressed them. He found them in a testy mood. Their mood was not improved by His Excellency's request that the House appropriate money to compensate those gentlemen whose property had been destroyed in the August riots, among whom were the detested Oliver and Hutchinson. Sensing the legislators' anger, Bernard decided that the best course was to send them home lest they act in some untoward fashion. He prorogued them until the end of October.

While members of the Massachusetts House waited to reappear in Boston, on 7 October at New York City, delegates to the Stamp Act Congress were taking their seats. Otis made a bid for chairmanship of the congress, but he was passed over;

in his stead the members elected Timothy Ruggles, the man Bernard had wriggled into the delegation.

For 12 days, the congress debated the rights of the American colonies. It was, for the most part, a temperate affair. In the end the congress drafted 13 resolutions, intoduced by a preamble expressing the body's "warmest Sentiments of Affection and Duty to his Majesty's Person and Government." Philosophically all agreed that Parliament had no right to tax Americans. Taxes could be levied only by colonial assemblies, the sole legal representatives of the people. The members made no distinction, as some writers later did, between internal and external taxes. Having excised the power of taxation, however, the congress was less certain about the residue of parliamentary authority. Precisely what sovereignty did Parliament exercise in America? That question, for the moment at least, was left open.

On 23 October, Bernard reconvened the General Court. Buoyed by the news from New York, and with less than one week before the Stamp Act was to go into effect, the court moved quickly to make its voice heard. Increasingly that voice belonged to Samuel Adams, whose rhetorical skills, learned at Harvard and honed in the press, were put to good use writing resolutions damning the Stamp Act and defending American rights. Not only did Adams become the official voice of the House; he was the informal one as well. Having to elicit support for their cause, members turned to him to write to influential friends in London and elsewhere on their behalf.

When the dreaded day of 1 November arrived, church bells tolled, flags were lowered to half mast, and Boston lamented the outrage of the Stamp Duty. Otherwise, however, a strange calm descended on the town. Ebenezer MacIntosh and his South End gang took to the streets, but only to parade peacefully and visit the Liberty Tree, where due observances were made. Such demonstrations of good order, by such disorderly men, were a worry to the authorities, for by keeping the rabble-rousers in line the Sons of Liberty were flaunting their power. All the governor could do was wait.

Perhaps to remind the royal governor precisely who controlled the streets of Boston, on 17 December the Sons arranged a meeting. The unfortunate Andrew Oliver was to be their guest. Although Oliver had already resigned as stamp master some were concerned that now that stamps were available, he might have second thoughts under pressure from the government. At the scheduled meeting, to be held under the Liberty Tree at noon, Oliver was invited to publicly resign his post again.

On the morning of the seventeenth, a "multitude," led by the indomitable MacIntosh, met Oliver at his home and escorted him to the appointed site. It was a "rainy and tempestuous day" as Oliver stood under the bare branches of the tree and again assured his fellow townsmen that he would never distribute stamps.

That winter, riots and resignations were common throughout the colonies. Wherever citizens organized in opposition, royal government was forced to give way. Authority could function only with consent, and Americans would not consent to the Stamp Act. Despite the provisions of the law, business proceeded as usual and stamps were ignored.

Tumults in America might have been more easily dismissed by the ministry and Parliament had they not been under pressure from their own constituents—the London merchants. Having watched their trade decline because of postwar readjustments, and aggravated by the Sugar Act, the empire's entrepreneurs were deeply concerned that the Stamp Act was simply another ill-conceived measure whose inevitable consequence was economic ruin. In New York, Philadelphia, and Boston, American merchants had signed agreements to boycott British goods until the act was repealed. Whether such agreements could be effective was not yet proven, but London merchants wished to avoid the trial.

Grenville had ignored the protests and warnings from America. He could not, however, ignore similar messages from constituents at home. By early 1766, it was clear the Stamp Act had failed and must be repealed. Repeal was one thing, appeasement quite another. Grenville and his minions had foolishly invested the Stamp Act with a burden of symbolic import. Thanks to their rhetoric, the issue now centered on a debate about parliamentary supremacy. Unconditional surrender was out of the question. Many members of Parliament questioned the wisdom of the act, although none questioned its constitutionality.

Having helped create a mess, Grenville was not responsible for cleaning it up. He had been replaced by the Marquis of Rockingham. Rockingham's challenge was to find a way to repeal the act and save face. Early in 1766 just such a scheme was hatched. In February the ministry introduced two measures, inextricably tied to one another. The first was the Declaratory Act, which boldly stated that Parliament was supreme in all matters whatsoever; the second repealed the Stamp Act.

In Boston the town rejoiced over the repeal. No one seemed to notice the Declaratory Act. "Words are but wind," noted the English satirist Samuel Butler. His observation could be applied to the Declaratory Act.

Adams and his colleagues, lawyers, cordwainers, merchants, and farmers had stood together, defied royal authority, and triumphed. The Sons of Liberty were heroes. Emboldened by their success, they and their friends stood ready to answer the next call to defend American rights.

CHAPTER 6

Townshend and Troops

❖
❖

Samuel Adams was not a person to be denied. Having helped put the royal government to flight over the Stamp Act, he was determined to continue the chase. In May 1766 his fellow members of the House nudged him toward that goal by electing him clerk.

Adams was the perfect choice for the post. His talents for organization and writing could be put to good use. Aside from the normal functions of record keeping, the clerk was also charged, under the general direction of the House, with communicating with the province's agent in London as well as with other assemblies in America. With his facile pen, Adams skewered enemies and extolled friends. He even arranged that henceforth votes would be taken by names, so that enemies to liberty might be more easily identified. It was also Adams who led the movement to install a gallery in the House chamber. He knew oratory was always more radical than the printed word. Peter Oliver saw precisely what Adams had in mind and accused him of filling the viewing stands with "Mohawks and Hawcubites, to echo the oppositional Vociferations, to the Rabble without Doors." There incendiary accusations hurled about within doors spread like wildfire without.

The same session that elected Adams clerk elevated Thomas Cushing to speaker. Cushing was the son of "Death's Head" Cushing, Adams's first mentor. He was a graduate of Harvard, class of 1744, a fellow member of the Old South, and a neighbor. Cushing and Adams were joined in the chamber by the increasingly unreliable Otis and by a new face in Boston politics, John Hancock.

For all their political lives, Hancock's and Adams's fates would be intertwined. Two apocryphal stories that enjoy an undying currency bear repeating. One has Adams, a few days before the election of new representatives, discussing candidates with other members of the caucus. As they drew a finger down the list of possibilities, many stopped at the name of John Rowe, a prominent merchant and Son of Liberty. Some spoke for Rowe, but Adams reputedly asked cryptically, "Is there not another John that may do better?" Turning his eyes toward Hancock's Beacon Hill mansion, he signaled the riddle's answer for those not clever enough to puzzle it out.

The other story is set on Election Day itself. Samuel and his cousin from Braintree, John Adams, were strolling across the Common, near Hancock's home, when Samuel remarked, "The town has done a wise thing today, . . . They have made that young man's fortune their own."

Like most stories of this sort, there was some truth in the images portrayed: Hancock, the vain idle young man with no particular skills but a large inherited fortune and a craving for fame; Adams, the political manipulator, cunning and sly, seeing in his protégé a political milch cow. Although no one can deny that Hancock was vain and Adams cunning, their relationship was more symbiotic than parasitic. Hancock was no fool. Adams was tutor, not creator.

Compared to the spring session's pyrotechnics over the Stamp Act, the fall meeting of the General Court was tame. There was, of course, the usual sniping between the governor and the House, led by Adams and Cushing, but with the Stamp Act buried, no great issue loomed. Parliament and the House were still unyielding in their contradictory views of the doctrine of absolute supremacy, but neither body, for the time being at least, had the spirit to challenge the other openly.

For the ministry the crisis would never be over until they found sufficient revenue, and that quest, when directed from London, would always lead to America. Despite all its bombastic rhetoric, the Declaratory Act would not raise a farthing.

Throughout the first half of 1767, rumors of new parliamentary taxes circulated in Boston. They had their origin in a remark made by Charles Townshend, the new chancellor of the exchequer. A rising star in the ministry, Townshend had boasted in January that he had a scheme to raise a revenue in America "free from offense." Everyone, on both sides of the Atlantic, awaited this miracle. Having made the promise Townshend then remained silent.

"Champagne" Charlie, a sobriquet Townshend earned from his reputed ability to deliver eloquent speeches while dead drunk, should have swallowed his boast. It only made him vulnerable to his opponents in Parliament who had a plan to force his hand. They managed to slide through a bill reducing the land tax, which naturally opened the gates on even more red ink. Townshend had no choice but to present his plan.

Townshend's scheme, remarkable for its unremarkableness, was a series of barely disguised taxes to be levied on a wide variety of goods imported into the colonies. Among the items to be saddled with duties were paper, paint, tea, and lead. Townshend, and many of his colleagues, mistakenly believed that Americans would accept these duties, since they fell into the category of an "external tax," that is, a duty on goods rather than a direct tax on individuals. The distinction was meaningless. The bill, commonly referred to as the Townshend Act, passed easily. It would raise, according to the treasury, barely £40,000, but it established a precedent that could be enlarged upon. The men in Parliament were comforted. The men of Boston were enraged.

Before the storm broke, Townshend died. Just as Rockingham had inherited a whirlwind from Grenville, so Townshend's successor Lord North faced the delicate problem of collecting duties. Building on past failures, Townshend had foreseen the problem and embedded in his act a provision for a separate board of customs commissioners based in America. While a separate board made sense politically, it was still risky; it became disastrously so when the ministry elected to situate the five-member board in Boston.

Bernard, Hutchinson, and Adams, in particular, understood the folly of sending the commissioners to Boston. Surely everyone could see that five bureaucrats standing against a whole community, "supported" by a royal government that only a few months previous had shown itself totally incapable of maintaining order, was madness. The ministry was backing itself into a corner. If Bostonians took to the streets, and who could doubt that they would, the government would face either retreat, an unlikely possibility, or enforcement. The latter course meant the dispatch of troops.

At town meeting, in the newspapers, and in his letters, Adams warned that the Townshend duties were mere preface to much more stringent acts. American liberties would be undermined. Revenue from the duties would allow Parliament to settle an army among them to enforce even more obnoxious acts. A horde of placemen would descend on the colonies to feed upon them. Adams even raised the horrid spectacle of an Anglican bishop resident on this side of the Atlantic, precisely the situation his ancestors had sought to escape.

In November the commissioners arrived. Their timing was abysmal. They stepped onto Long Wharf on 5 November, Pope's Day. The town, as traditionally befitted the day, was in an uproar. Undoubtedly a bit nervous, for there was no one present to offer them protection, the commissioners walked up King Street.

Determined to serve notice on the commissioners in a manner they would not likely forget, Adams saw to it that the mob took to the streets, cudgels in hand and bonfires blazing. Not a hair on the head of even one commissioner was disturbed. On this occasion the mob was deployed to intimidate not destroy. According to one account, the "boys" were disappointed that they had not been able to draw the commissioners into their "frolic"; nonetheless, they obeyed their instructions. The Sons of Liberty were willing to wait.

In the interim, Adams was laying plans for the upcoming winter session of the House. He was also beginning to promote the tactic of a boycott. Although the strategy of nonimportation had been bandied about during the Stamp Act protest, it had not really been tested, since the measure had been repealed so quickly.

Like the phoenix, nonimportation rose again inspired by the Townshend threat. When Adams stood in town meeting and urged his fellow citizens to boycott British imports, he did so not so much to obstruct the collection of new duties—that was a momentary issue, ephemeral and likely to change—but rather because he felt deeply that his community had gone sadly astray.

Adams was a romantic. His view of history was heroic, and his heroes were drawn from the Roman republic and Massachusetts Bay. In the glorious days of the Roman senate, the republic had been ruled by noble and virtuous men whose only concern was to serve the interests of the state. The republic fell when vice, a lust for power and riches, displaced the noble aims of the men in the Forum.

The early days of Massachusetts were similarly an heroic age, for virtuous men and women had braved a howling wilderness to build a community under the rule of God's law. In succeeding generations, much had changed, and, in Adams's view, not for the better. "Men," he said, "should have no ruling Passion but the Love of their Country." Like the prophets of the Old Testament, he identified virtue with simplicity and frugality, yet all around him he saw worrisome signs of declension—extravagant homes, elegant clothes, a dazzling social life, luxuries proliferating everywhere. All were outward signs of inner decay. Virtue appeared to be in retreat.

To Adams and those who shared his view, the flight of virtue was not simply a spiritual matter. Liberty and virtue were the twin pillars supporting a free society, and without its companion, liberty would crumble into dust. Only a government of virtuous men could be trusted to respect the rights of its citizens. Only a virtuous people would be able to resist the sinister encroachments of a corrupt British ministry.

Adams's alchemy was to bring virtue, liberty, and nonimportation into a potent mix that could excite popular attention. In the House, at town meeting, through broadsides, letters, and newspapers, Adams drove home his view of politics. Those who opposed him opposed liberty and virtue. Such degenerate men, governments, and institutions were outside the pale and could lawfully be destroyed. By this logic, it was possible for Adams and those who agreed with him, to attack the homes of their enemies, humiliate them in public, and, if repentance were not forthcoming, to take yet stronger measures, even to the point of revolution. It was Adams's genius, perhaps even his obsession, never to waver from this view. Depending on circumstances, those around him might waver and fall by the wayside, but Adams never yielded.

It would be difficult to find among Adams's contemporaries any who matched him in his selfless devotion to public service. Above all, he strove to be an agent of public virtue in what he saw as an increasingly corrupt world. At the center of that mission was his sense of covenant, a sacred, energizing concept that had been carried from the Old World to the new by his Puritan ancestors. Massachusetts's fading glory could be recaptured, he believed, if its citizens rallied round in a new covenant to resist the efforts of a corrupt regime bent on undermining American virtue. Nonimportation was a means of acting on that covenant.

Adams's initial efforts at nonimportation were not particularly successful. Town meeting resolved "to encourage industry and economy" to promote domestic manufactures, and to boycott imported luxuries. But violations were legion. Moreover, when Boston sent out letters asking other towns to join the boycott, the response was negligible. To Adams's dismay, Boston and America lacked the spirit to do more than grumble at the Townshend duties.

Adams need not have worried, however. Whenever benign neglect might have served to calm political passions in the colonies, royal officials in London and Boston sprang into action. Invariably the measures taken proved counterproductive. Early in 1768 officials were poised on the threshold of another blunder.

January 1768 was a busy time. The House had convened for its winter session, and Clerk Adams was hard at work keeping records and writing official letters. On the twelfth a letter was dispatched to the province's agent in London, Dennys De Berdt. Three days later another to the Earl of Shelburne, and on the twentieth one to the king himself. All these letters were similar in tone—they pledged loyalty but strongly protested the new duties. On 22 January, however, the House exercised its power of oversight on the zealous clerk. Adams and his allies had proposed that a letter be circulated among the other colonial assemblies asking them to join with Massachusetts in opposing the Townshend Acts. To the more conservative delegates, mostly from rural areas, this went too far, and the letter was put aside. On the morrow matters returned to an orderly state, and within a few days more respectful letters were sent to the Marquis of Rockingham, Lord Camden, and William Pitt, now Lord Chatham.

With the exception of the withdrawn circular letter, Adams had little faith that any of his epistolary efforts would have much effect. Indeed, according to family history, one morning as Adams was preparing to leave home his daughter exclaimed with awe that the letter he was carrying was likely to be touched by the king's hands. Her father retorted that it was far more likely to be trod upon by the royal foot.

Although defeated, on the twenty-second Adams knew how to bide his time. He was well aware of his colleagues' habits and knew how to use them to his advantage. Representatives who traveled to Boston from distant places such as Worcester and Hampshire Counties were always bemoaning the expense of living in Boston and the separation from their families and businesses. Ever anxious to be done with proceedings, many departed before the formal end of the session. By the second week of February, a number of members were on the road home. Counting the empty chairs, Adams reintroduced the circular letter on 11 February. This time it passed overwhelmingly.

The letter was addressed to the speakers of the other colonial assemblies. While respectful, it was also firm. The opening lines set the tone. The Massachusetts House had, according to the letter, "taken into serious Consideration, the great difficultys that must accrue to themselves & their Constituents by the operation of several acts of Parliament imposing Duties & Taxes on the American Colonies." The chief difficulty, according to Adams, was that the acts violated the "fundamental Rules of the British Constitution," chief among them "that what a man has honestly acquired is absolutely his own, which he may freely give, but cannot be taken from him without his consent." Since "the People of this province" were not represented in Parliament the recent acts taxing them were unconstitutional.

The letter proceeded to explain why it was impossible, both practically and philosophically, for the colonies to be represented in Parliament. Adams was also quick to assert that the duties and taxes were not the only troubling measures imposed by London. He specifically referred to a declaration that judges in Massachusetts were now to be paid from the royal treasury. By thus making judges "independent of the people," Adams queried, "hath not [London introduced] a tendency to subvert the principles of Equity & endanger the Happiness and Security of the Subject"? Among the judges taking the king's pay was Adams's old nemesis, Thomas Hutchinson.

Judges, of course, were not the only servants of the king residing in Boston. Adams called attention to the fact that the recently arrived customs commissioners were authorized to appoint any number of lesser officers to serve them. This threatened to multiply "officers of the Crown . . . to such a degree as to become dangerous to the Liberty of the people." As soon as copies of the letter were made, it was on its way to the other colonies.

Adams said less than he might have in the circular letter. He did not completely deny, for example, the authority of Parliament. Despite his own convictions, he was careful not to step out too far ahead of others. Governor Bernard, however, saw no moderation in the letter. It was in his eyes an infamous document and its circulation a singular personal embarrassment. For the effrontery to his position he prorogued the General Court.

It was a miserable spring for the governor. Writing for the newspapers under the pseudonym "Puritan," Adams railed about bishops and popery, trying as best he could to link the governor and his friends with papist plots. Not a shred of evidence supported these attacks. Nonetheless, they resonated in Boston, where the specter of Catholicism could always be conjured up.

Adams's unrelenting attacks were not Bernard's only problem. On almost a daily basis, the governor had to listen to the incessant whining of the customs commissioners. Everywhere they went they were jeered at and threatened. In broad daylight brazen Bostonians carted smuggled goods through the streets right under their noses. Such disdain dare not be tolerated, and the commissioners demanded that Bernard ask for troops to enforce the royal laws. Bernard soothed his nervous friends, but for the moment he would not ask for troops. By the end of March, the commissioners, tired of His Excellency's unresponsiveness, wrote directly to London for assistance.

Resistance to customs officers was hardly a novelty anywhere in the British empire, so it is likely the ministry was not overly concerned with the seemingly exaggerated reports of a few men in Boston. In June, however, the customs commissioners found something to report that not even the ministry could easily dismiss.

Late in the afternoon of 9 May, *Liberty*, a small sloop owned by John Hancock and named in honor of John Wilkes, nosed her way past Boston Light, eased into the harbor, and came alongside Hancock's wharf. She was inbound from Madeira, under the command of Captain Marshall. Ordinarily the customs officers would have boarded immediately, but since it was sunset and the light was fast fading, they decided to wait until the morning.

That night, under Captain Marshall's direction, the crew worked overtime. The customs officers might have had trouble doing their job in the dark, but apparently Hancock's men did not. When the customs inspector returned the next morning, he found only 25 pipes of wine aboard, a mere fraction of what had been there only a few hours before. Not surprisingly, witnesses proved impossible to find.

Since the vessel belonged to Hancock, "a high son of liberty," the customs officers were dogged in their determination to find sufficient evidence to libel *Liberty.* It took the officers a month, but finally, through the influence of a few pounds and the threat of punishment, they found a witness who recounted how Hancock's men had smuggled the wine ashore. On 10 June the commissioners seized *Liberty,* but before they could take her to safety, 500 townsmen, alerted to what was happening, gathered at the wharf and pelted the officers with stones. The commissioners were then chased through the streets to their homes, where the mob proceeded to smash windows. Under cover of darkness, the commissioners fled to the safety of Castle William.

Hancock viewed the humiliation of the commissioners as sufficient punishment. An astute merchant, he was now concerned with securing his investment. On the day following the seizure and the riot he negotiated a deal that would return his vessel to him. When Adams learned of the agreement, he immediately visited Otis and Dr. Joseph Warren. What might be good for Hancock was clearly not good for Boston. To allow Hancock to deal with the commissioners would seriously undermine the patriot movement. On Sunday, 11 June, Adams, Otis, and Warren trudged up Beacon Hill to meet with Hancock. This Sabbath would not be a day of rest for the gentlemen. Over generous amounts of recently arrived Madeira, they persuaded Hancock that he had made a bad bargain. Dealing with the customs men implied concession. Better that he should stand on his rights and have nothing to do with the rascals. At midnight on Sunday, Dr. Warren rapped on the commissioner's office door to deliver the news. There would be no deal. In this poisoned atmosphere, Bernard received ominous instructions from Lord Hillsborough.

Time and time again, in sundry letters and petitions, Americans in nearly every colony had told the ministry how much they valued the power of their own assemblies. The line of sovereignty between Parliament and colonial assemblies was not precise, but there could be no quicker way to rouse Americans than to attack the independence of their representative government. This is exactly what the ministry did.

When the news arrived, Samuel Adams was both stunned and elated. Lord Hillsborough directed Governor Bernard to order the Massachusetts House to rescind the circular letter and expunge it from their record. In an equally terse manner, governors in other colonies were warned that their houses were not to approve the letter.

At precisely the moment when Adams was searching for kindling to fire opposition against the royal government, his lordship delivered him an ample supply. That the ministry should think they could compel the Massachusetts House to do anything was prima facie evidence of their ignorance of American history and politics.

By a vote of 92 to 17, the members of the House voted to defy the order from Lord Hillsborough. In their reply to the governor, penned in the hand of clerk Samuel Adams, the House refused to rescind the letter. The assembly then attacked His Excellency for misrepresenting the loyal people of Massachusetts to the king. Humiliated, Bernard watched as most of his own supporters deserted him to vote on the side of the patriots. The 17 "miscreants" soon had their names posted on the Liberty Tree as "parricides," doomed to burn in hell. In North Square the patriot silversmith Paul Revere applied his extraordinary craft to the work of fashioning a "Liberty Bowl" celebrating the brave 92 and damning the abominable 17.

In the days following the dispatch of the circular letter, Adams rejoiced as each mail brought positive reports from other colonies. Virginia, New Hampshire, and Connecticut echoed their support of Massachusetts Bay. It was for Adams a moment of redemption. Massachusetts may have been slow to rise against the Stamp Act, but now it had recaptured the lead from Virginia.

Having roused the House, Adams and his friends next turned their sights on the council. With the governor's followers scurrying for cover, Adams had little trouble wreaking havoc on that erstwhile conservative body. Intimidated by the threat of the populace, the council fell under the sway of the House leaders. The feckless Bernard reported to Hillsborough that the "Citadel" of royal government had capitulated.

As long as there was no force to maintain the king's law, "capitulation" was the only possible outcome of the contest in Boston. Repeatedly Bernard had tried to convince his superiors that troops were the answer. They had denied him. Now, as the pile of reports overspread his desk detailing the lawlessness of Bostonians grew higher, Hillsborough could ill afford to ignore Bernard's wisdom. Only the sight of redcoats and glistening bayonets could bring Bostonians to line. Two regiments of troops were ordered to Boston.

Rumors that troops were to be sent spiced preparations for the annual celebration of Andrew Oliver's resignation as stamp master. On the prior Monday Adams published a scorching essay in Edes and Gill's *Gazette*. It was intended, of course, to whip up enthusiasm for the coming event. Under the pen name "Determinatus," Adams railed against the perfidy of the governor and his wanton misrepresentation of the state of affairs in Boston. Bostonians were by nature, according to Adams, peaceable folk who unfortunately had been provoked to anger by the outrageous behavior of the commissioners. If the peace of the province had been interrupted it was not the fault of the people but of their governors. The people of Massachusetts were enlightened. They know how to distinguish, and I pray God they ever may, between the *due execution of the laws of the land,* and the exercise of *new, invented, strange, unconstitutional* Powers, repugnant to the British Constitution and the Charter of the Province. So deep rooted is their abhorrence of such powers as these, that I question whether civil, military or ecclesiastic authority united, will ever be sufficient to induce them to yield.

In the end, argued Adams, the people's grievances would either be addressed or they would "become poor deluded miserable ductile Dupes, fitted to be made the slaves of dirty tools of arbitrary power."

One week after the *Gazette* published Adams's incendiary piece, the Sons of Liberty gathered to commemorate 14 August. Among the honored guests was Samuel Adams. The day began with a ceremony at the sacred Liberty Tree. There the assembled sang songs of liberty and watched attentively while the artillery company fired a 14-gun salute. About noon, after numerous toasts, the most distinguished of the company repaired across Boston Neck to the Greyhound tavern in Roxbury where they continued feasting and drinking. Before ending the day, they stepped outside the tavern, and in a solemn moment, "consecrated a tree in the vicinity, under the shade of which, on some future anniversary, they may commemorate the day which shall liberate America from her present oppression."

Despite Adams's rhetoric, most Bostonians had yet to experience any "oppression." Indeed, as the past three years had shown, Bernard and company had much more to fear from Bostonians than Bostonians had to fear from the royal government. That was soon to change, for on 3 September, Governor Bernard quietly confirmed to one of his councilors that four regiments, two from Ireland and two from Halifax, were en route to Boston. Within minutes the news was on the streets.

CHAPTER 7

Boston Under Siege

❖
❖

Devotion to his community shaped Samuel Adams's views on nearly everything. But he was an eighteenth-century Englishman, and thus held certain notions about the manner in which to conduct politics. Despite the fiery rhetoric, of which he was a master, Adams was always careful to stay within defined limits. Personal assaults on the king or the promotion of violence, for example, were not permissible. Eighteenth-century Englishmen, Adams included, accepted certain genteel standards for public discourse.

Of course sometimes the public discourse might draw the less genteel into mayhem. But mob violence was street theater—staged, managed, and in its own way quite restrained. Mobs were selective, harm was not administered randomly, and almost none of the culprits were ever discovered and punished. Samuel Adams, Thomas Hutchinson, James Otis, Francis Bernard—all were of the Boston elite no matter what their political perspective—knew intuitively that there were bounds to behavior. Sending troops was decidedly beyond those bounds. Using glistening bayonets to prod Bostonians into obeying laws they believed unconstitutional was bound to cause trouble.

Although the quaking customs commissioners were nearly hysterical in their call for troops, other royal officials were less certain. Even the obtuse Bernard understood that redcoats in Boston were likely to incite further violence and stiffen patriot resolve. Only when making plans to leave Boston did the governor advocate dispatching troops to tame the "Saints." Others, like Thomas Hutchinson, who were rooted in the town, remained skeptical that redcoats and bayonets could restore order. Less than a year before, the lieutenant governor had written to his friend Richard Jackson that if Bostonians were inclined to obey Parliament, a token force of troops would be quite sufficient to keep peace. On the other hand, if they were determined to resist, according to Hutchinson, it would be "difficult to determine what number would be necessary to enforce obedience." The ministry performed its own calculations. It dispatched four regiments.

Rage was the response from Samuel Adams. Nothing the ministry, governor, Thomas Hutchinson, or any other henchman of the royal government had ever done struck at him so hard as the dispatch of troops. There was no subtlety here, no clever political manipulation, no discourse. This was pure, naked power. It smacked of military despotism of the worst sort. It violated Adams's deep sense of community and covenant that those with whom he had disputed, but with whom he believed he shared certain values, should willfully cast those values aside. In Adams's view the ministry had "let slip the dogs of war." Now he, too, was prepared to fling open the gates.

His homeland threatened by invasion, Adams threw off the restraint that normally characterized his public persona. What broke forth, for the moment at least, was passion worthy of a revolutionary. According to government informants, Adams was seen and heard throughout the town urging his fellow townsmen to arms. "If you are Men behave like Men; let us take up arms immediately and be free and Seize all the King's Officers: we shall have thirty thousand Men to join us from the Country." That Adams could utter such treason and still walk the streets of Boston provides insight into the power-lessness of the king's government in the province.

Early in September, the Boston selectmen instructed the town's constables to post warrants warning the inhabitants that a special town meeting was to be held on 12 September. The purpose of the meeting was to discuss measures to defend the town should it be attacked by the French! In anticipation of such an attack, the selectmen resurrected a province law rarely if ever used, and made provision to clean the ancient muskets stacked in the bowels of Faneuil Hall. The symbolism was apparent to all.

On 12 September, amid a swirl of rumors that the Sons of Liberty were secretly laying plans to seize Castle William, town meeting convened. With Adams clearly in control, the meeting passed a resolution asking the governor to convene the House. When he wisely refused, the meeting voted several strongly worded resolutions and issued a call for a special convention where towns could discuss the grave matters facing the province.

Just as the cleaning of weapons was intended to convey a serious message, so too was the use of the word *convention*. In 1660 a "convention" in England restored Charles II to the throne. In 1689 a "convention" had completed the "Glorious Revolution" by installing William and Mary on the throne. In that same year Edmund Andros, governor of the Dominion of New England, had been deposed by a "convention" meeting in Boston. To eighteenth-century Englishmen the word *convention* meant change.

Sixty-seven towns sent representatives to the meeting, which gathered in Faneuil Hall on 22 September. Boston named Adams, Cushing, Hancock, and Otis, the same delegation that sat in the House. Most towns followed the same principle. Indeed, House speaker Cushing was chosen as chair of the convention and Adams its clerk. In nearly every way, except in the eyes of the law, this was a meeting of the House. Here was a precedent for a meeting of provincial government without the approbation of the governor.

For nearly a week, the convention met and debated the issues. Resolutions were passed and sent to the governor (he rejected them), and letters were approved to be sent to various people in England. Contrary to what Adams had hoped, it had turned out to be a reasonably moderate affair. Toward the end of the meeting on the twenty-seventh, news arrived in the hall that several troop transports had passed Boston Light and were coming to anchor at Kings Roads.

On Friday morning, 30 September, Adams learned that small boats with their sailors heaving the lead line were moving about the inner harbor. There was only one explanation for such activity; the sailors were taking soundings to find the best anchorage for their ships. In the afternoon, nearly a dozen warships came up close to the town and dropped anchor, their broadsides facing the town. Before long, troopships followed in their wake. Boston was under siege.

On Saturday the troops landed. Leaving their transports behind, the longboats made their rhythmic way toward Long Wharf, guarded by warships with open gun ports and shotted cannon. Several times the small boats shuttled back and forth, hauling their cargo to the wharf. Each time, more soldiers scrambled forth and fell into ranks, until the regiments and their train of artillery were assembled and ready to march. The bands struck up a martial tune, flags were unfurled, and, with a quick step, the troops set off up King Street. Bostonians were impressed, but not cowed. Adams summed up the feelings of most when, under the pen name "Vindex," he wrote in the *Boston Gazette,* "Will the spirits of people as yet unsubdued by tyranny, unaw'd by the menaces of arbitrary power, submit to be *govern'd* by military force? No."

Soldiers were everywhere. With more than a thousand redcoats garrisoning the town, Bostonians stumbled into them everywhere. They saw them drilling on the Common, standing guard duty at the customs house, and in the evening milling about the streets and taverns. This was the "standing army" so often mentioned as a threat to liberty. How often in history had soldiers been used by despots to enforce their will on the people? But if the soldiers presented a threat to liberty they also bid to undermine the morals of the town.

Always concerned to preserve their virtue, Bostonians looked upon these young soldiers as dregs and vermin let loose among them in a veritable plot by the devil. In this the people of Boston shared a view common to eighteenth-century Englishmen. Indeed, there was an oft spoken aphorism: "Messmate before a shipmate, shipmate before a friend, friend before a dog, dog before a soldier." Hard pressed to fill their ranks, British regiments were none too careful about who put on the king's colors and shouldered a musket. The army was filled with men whose only other choices were either the hangman or jail.

In a society that read and prayed, the two most important purveyors of information were printers and preachers. In Boston both professions were overwhelmingly patriot in sympathy. Together the printing presses and the pulpits of the town spewed forth a continuous flow of venom aimed at the government and what they perceived as its evil policies.

Chief among the practitioners of the pulpit was Adams's friend and ally Samuel Cooper. Brother to town clerk William Cooper, Samuel was minister at the Brattle Street Church where he counted among his parishioners a number of influential Bostonians including John Hancock and, on occasion, Samuel Adams.

Cooper's profession was the ministry, but his love was politics. In 1753 "Silver-Tongued Sam" was appointed chaplain to the House of Representatives, a post where he was quite able to mingle "religion and politics so skillfully that he became the moral vindication of the policies of the Whigs." With his silky tones and sense of the dramatic, Cooper managed to sway his congregation. He was in the habit of wearing an elaborate cassock—"one sleeve would make a full trimm'd negligee"—which gave him an almost Romish appearance. In fact, one old communicant remarked that he suspected Cooper had a pope in his belly. In private conversation he was just as awesome, and those who met him came away impressed by the apparent breadth of his learning.

From his pulpit, Cooper railed against religious tyranny (the Anglican church) and political oppression (the British ministry). His own liberality and that of most of his congregation allowed for the intrusion of a good measure of secularization, and Cooper himself is reported to have remarked once that "an ounce of mother's wit is worth a pound of clergy." As a member of Boston's black legion he was, in the words of John Adams, an "excellent hand to spread a rumor."

Rumors spread from the pulpit fell only on those within earshot. Newspapers had a far greater reach than the spoken word. This was a medium in which Samuel Adams was particularly adept.

Adams was always writing. Between the arrival of the troops in October 1768 and August 1769, for example, he wrote ten letters to officials on both sides of the Atlantic. During the same period he also authored at least twenty newspaper articles under the pen names Candidus and Vindex. While these letters and articles circulated widely, their readership was relatively limited. Candidus, Vindex, and the clerk of the House argued at a cerebral level with a vocabulary shared by an educated elite. Their arguments made their way down to the wharves and into the taverns but only after the issues and words had been rephrased in simpler language to make them more intelligible to the masses.

Repeatedly Adams had shown his willingness and skill in reaching the lower classes. In Tory circles his frequent visits to taverns had earned him the nickname "Sam the Publican." Beginning shortly after the arrival of the troops Adams showed just how versatile his pen could be with *A Journal of the Times*.

In its inaugural issue, dated 13 October 1768, the authors claimed that everything contained in its pages was "strictly fact." Not everyone agreed. Thomas Hutchinson told all who would listen that "Nine tenths of the *Journal* is either absolutely false or grossly misrepresented." No one, however, disputed the fact that the *Journal* made fascinating reading as it chronicled the daily affairs of Boston, a town under siege.

This was tabloid journalism at its sensational best. Twin themes ran through every issue. The first was the incalculable harm being done to the "innocent" citizens of Boston by the "despicable" soldiers. Citizens were beaten in the street. "A tradesman on his way home had a thrust in the breast with a bayonet from a soldier." Night watchmen making their rounds were assaulted by drunken redcoats. On another occasion, when a "householder hearing the cries of two women in the night, who were rudely treated by some soldiers," tried to come to their aid, "he was knocked down with a musket and much wounded." Later a woman of the North End brought charges of rape against a soldier who "made his escape." Almost as if to emphasize the baseness of their men, regimental commanders had offenders flogged (usually by black drummers) on the Common, and in one instance they held an execution by firing squad. Even in eighteenth-century Boston, a place not unaccustomed to the spectacle of public punishment, these scenes drew attention and underscored the brutality of the citizenry's oppressors.

A second theme resonating through the *Journal* centered on the other agents of the king, the much despised commissioners of the customs. With their near vice regal authority, the commissioners could act outside the normal structure of colonial government. Working through the admiralty courts they could circumvent the provincial legal system. Even the royal governor could not have interfered with their work. Immediately upon arriving in Boston, the commissioners pieced together a network of agents to snoop, inform, and enforce the customs laws. Not loathe to use their power to reward friends and punish enemies, the commissioners were an easy target for the *Journal*. Nearly every issue carried some revelation that discredited both the law and the enforcement officials. In the pages of the *Journal* Bostonians were always innocent; the commissioners were always guilty.

By writing anonymously the authors hoped to avoid discovery and possible prosecution. Anonymity, however, also gave greater credibility to the lurid stories. For if the authors had signed their contributions, the purpose and bias of the accounts would have been abundantly clear. Of course, presented with such a puzzle, few could resist trying to sort it out.

Governor Bernard thought Samuel Adams was the chief author. He may well have been. Adams's surviving papers make no mention whatsoever of the *Journal*. Such a conspicuous absence for such an important effort seems decidedly deliberate. Others have sent the credit to William Cooper, Boston's town clerk and brother to Samuel Cooper. Cooper too may have been involved, but some of the essays possess detail and analysis beyond what was available to the town clerk.

Although clearly written in Boston, the *Journal* was printed in New York, an additional protection for authors. Material appears to have been collected and dispatched on Saturdays. Other evidence exists which suggests that on Saturdays, Adams, Otis, Cooper, and others were likely to be found at the shop of Edes and Gill. Taken together these circumstances strongly indicate that on Saturdays Adams and company gathered to write and edit the *Journal*.

As propaganda the *Journal* was a phenomenal success. Produced in Boston and printed in New York, the tales of Boston's woes appeared a few days later in Philadelphia's *Pennsylvania Chronicle* and from there they spread throughout the colonies, eventually finding their way into the London papers. "The *Journal* was the most sustained effort to spread ideas through news items that was made in the entire twenty years" leading up to the Revolution. People in America came to believe that Boston, indeed, was a town under siege. To put faith in the *Journal* was to know that the frontier of American liberty was on the banks of the Charles River. Bostonians were brave and stoic citizens defiantly standing in defense of the rights of all Americans. The message was clear—should the ministry succeed in Boston, other American communities would soon succumb.

It was important for Adams to portray Bostonians as united, but that was not the case. Most of the divisions centered on the issue of nonimportation.

With Adams leading the way on 28 October 1767, the town meeting had met to consider "measures for economy and frugality to lessen the consumption and importation of European manufactured goods." Even though many merchants present at the meeting were skeptical, the measure passed easily, and soon a subscription was circulated to which all were invited to append their signatures. Later the same subscription was carried door to door.

Naturally the *Gazette* proclaimed that the nonimportation agreement was a success; that judgment, though, must be questioned. Of Boston's two hundred or so merchants, about eighty were known allies of Adams; the remainder simply wanted to continue business as usual. Others like the Hutchinsons and Olivers, however, were friends of the governor. Although Adams could always get a vote out of the town meeting, the merchants were not a group within his control.

It took nearly five months of "persuasion" to get the body of merchants to agree to nonimportation. Adams's strategy was to pack the merchants' association with his friends and allies. On 14 March when the merchants gathered to discuss the issue, among their company, according to Thomas Hutchinson, was a large number of "forestallers, retailers, pedlars, milliners, hawkers, squeezers and grinders." Hutchinson was probably close to the mark. Subsequently, to no one's surprise, the assembled "merchants" agreed to nonimportation, which would take effect on 1 June and continue until 31 December 1769. Adams's victory was not entirely complete. There were still some reluctant subscribers who managed to attach a proviso that Boston's nonimportation must hinge on New York and Philadelphia merchants adopting similar measures.

These men were not fools. If they were to lose money by adhering to nonimportation, their competitors in New York and Philadelphia could not be allowed to profit at their expense. At best, securing their agreement would delay nonimportation; at worst, the other towns could scuttle the strategy entirely. To his relief, Adams received good news from New York that summer; Philadelphia followed suit a few months later.

Nonimportation was only a small item in Samuel Adams's ultimate plan. Most Americans assumed that the pressure of nonimportation would send London merchants screaming to Parliament to lift the duties. While that scenario would satisfy most Americans, it did not satisfy Samuel Adams.

Nonimportation was, in Adams's view, just the tip of the wedge. He argued that nonimportation would free the colonies of their groveling economic dependence on the mother country. As a staunch Puritan Adams urged repeatedly that luxuries and superfluities be eschewed. There could be no tea drinking and extravagant clothes. Americans should turn to each other for all they needed. He delighted in the news that the graduates of his alma mater took their degrees wearing clothes that were made at home. He urged Cooper and other members of the clergy "to preach up Manufactures instead of Gospel." His radical friend Thomas Young even went so far as to suggest that Yankee farmers cut down their stands of oak and pasture sheep which would supply wool enough to clothe everyone in the colonies.

If America should become, in Adams's words, a "Great Empire," what would become of the mother country? If economic independence was attained, what would tie America to Britain? Adams went to the brink but stopped. Given how he felt about Parliament and the king it seems likely he was ready to follow economic independence with its political analog. Others were not ready, however. Always a bit ahead, but never out of sight of his followers, Adams understood that for the moment, at least, advocacy of nonimportation and self-reliance must stand on their own merits; additional implications could not be forced.

All of Adams's enemies and many of his friends thought he was impossibly naive in economics. Otis was quick to point out that whereas America had abundant natural resources, its labor supply was limited and expensive. Bernard called self-reliance "the idlest Bully that ever was attempted to be imposed upon sensible People." Adams persisted. He was convinced that the spirit of the people would make up for any shortage of material resources.

Nonimportation was not only a means toward economic independence, it was also a rallying point for those wishing to lodge their protest. In Boston and elsewhere, committees of inspection were appointed to ferret out the unfaithful who violated the agreement. Such transgression was not simply an error in judgment but was tantamount to heresy, a sin that carried with it both the threat of punishment and the promise of redemption. Those caught were first publicly humiliated (in rare cases physically punished), and then given the opportunity to repent and rejoin society.

This age-old covenant philosophy was at the heart of Adams's concept of nonimportation, and he was eager to extend it throughout America. He was encouraged mightily when, by the end of 1769, almost all the colonies from New Hampshire to Georgia had joined in the cause. "One spirit," he wrote, "animates all America . . . to *quench* the spirit, all the colonies must be absolutely *destroyed*." His optimism was premature. He had refused to acknowledge that even in Boston, the patriot stronghold, cracks in nonimportation were beginning to appear.

For decades Bostonians of all political stripes had made a science of deceiving royal customs officials. With that sort of experience, evading nonimportation posed few challenges. Tories such as Thomas Hutchinson and his sons made no pretense of self-denial and thus suffered the opprobrium of the town. Others, however, were far more duplicitous in public, pretending to be town loyal supporters while secretly enjoying banned goods.

Adams could recognize who among his friends were playing foul, but in an ironic twist of fate he was forced to protect them. If it should become widely known that certain patriots were more interested in money than principle, then the town would be disgraced, its moral leadership impugned and nonimportation jeopardized. To Adams it was better to tolerate a few wayward patriots than suffer such a failure. One such wayward patriot was John Hancock.

Samuel Adams and John Hancock were the proverbial odd couple. In appearance alone they stood apart: Adams rumpled, overweight, and rather uncaring about his personal dress; Hancock attractive and always nattily attired. Although the son and grandson of ministers, Hancock located his world in the countinghouse, not the meetinghouse. Adams was far more puritanical in his philosophy. Thoughtful and reflective he had a capacity to plunge into himself. Hancock preferred to skate across life's surfaces.

Hancock was an important merchant, a member of the social elite. He resented Parliament's acts because they hurt his business. But just as annoying was the insulting and disdainful treatment he, as a colonial, suffered from snobbish British aristocrats. His alienation from England was both personal and financial.

For his own reasons, Adams had also come to loathe the English. Like Hancock, he, and his father as well, had been ill treated by the English, but his disenchantment was more profound than Hancock's. Adams was fundamentally and absolutely opposed to any power that sought to impose itself upon the people. Sovereignty rested not in some distant place and with strangers. Sovereignty must reside with the people. Hancock's opposition to Parliament was particular and confined to specific acts; Adams's opposition was all-encompassing. Adams's worldview was inimical to concepts of possessive individualism and extravagant consumption. For him the community as a whole was more important than the individual and that community could be judged by how well it drew itself together in defense of simplicity and virtue.

Hancock's relativism and aristocratic habits encouraged him to be selective in his observance of nonimportation. In all likelihood, however, his sins did not exceed those of many other patriot merchants; he was simply more visible than most.

The man who cast a light on the shadowy dealings of Hancock and his fellow patriot merchants was John Mein, printer of the *Boston Chronicle* and the town's enfant terrible. His close connections to custom officers gave him access to the manifest of every vessel arriving in port. Not only were these lists revealing, they were embarrassing. In one instance, Hancock appeared as the consignee of a cargo of canvas that, upon closer examination, had the feel of fine linens. With Adams all the while preaching frugality and simplicity, Mein announced gleefully that Hancock had just taken delivery on an ornate and elegant carriage, hardly a sign of simple living.

Patriots squirmed as the *Chronicle* ripped the cloak of righteousness from them. Other Tory newspapers in Philadelphia, Newport, and New York were only too eager to reprint Mein's muckraking columns that so beautifully unmasked Boston's hypocrisy. With each new story Mein shattered another piece of patriot respectability. He had to be silenced.

It is true, Adams was troubled by Hancock's behavior, and indeed the behavior of a good portion of the merchant community. But unity, or at least its appearance, was at the moment of prime importance. It became clear to Mein he was a marked man. He took to seclusion and when he moved about, carried a pistol. On the evening of 28 October 1769, he was spotted by a gang of roving men who taunted, "Kill him, kill him." He barely escaped the gang by reaching the sanctuary of the guard house. The crowd would not be denied its pleasure, though. Having missed Mein, they found another quarry, George Geyer, a suspected customs informer. Geyer "was stripped naked, put in a Cart where he was first tarred, then feathered," and in this condition carried through the principal streets of the town followed by a great concourse of people. Mein, like poor Geyer, had by his actions put himself beyond the protection of the community and now suffered the consequences.

Geyer's fate and Mein's close escape were symptoms of an evil turn of affairs in Boston. Violence was becoming commonplace, a development most dramatically highlighted on the evening of 5 September at the British Coffee House. A customs officer, named John Robinson, and James Otis got into a brawl. By all accounts, Otis took the worst of the beating, a battering that pushed his delicate mind closer to the brink of insanity. The town flew into a rage and forced Robinson to flee to England. Otis never fully recovered from the blows, and in the months to come, his mind slipped slowly into dementia.

Adams fretted. Despite their best efforts at persuasion and intimidation, he and the Sons had not been fully able to stop the flow of trade into the town. In only a few weeks, on the final day of the year, nonimportation would be over as all had agreed. It was an open secret that several merchants had already sent their spring orders over to London. Making matters worse, at least from Adams's perspective, was the faint promise that in the spring Parliament would repeal the duties. He believed this was nothing more than a clever ploy on the part of the ministry to further undermine American resolve. As the new year drew nigh Adams feared that all he had accomplished was in peril.

Resentful that merchants should desert the cause, Adams railed at them in the *Gazette*. "We hear them [i.e., the merchants] very gravely asking, Have we not a right to carry on our own trade and sell our own goods if we please? who shall hinder us? This is now the language of those who had before seen the ax laid at the very root of *all* our *Rights* with apparent *complacency*." Mocking them he asked, "Have you not a right if you please, to set fire to your own houses, because they are your own, tho in all probability it will destroy a whole neighbourhood, perhaps a whole city!" He went on to challenge,

> Where did you learn that in a state or society you had a right to do as you please? Be pleased to be informed that you are bound to conduct yourselves as the Society with which you are joined are pleased to have you conduct, or if you please, you may leave it. It is true the will and pleasure of the society is generally declared in its laws: But there may be exceptions, and the present case is without doubt one.

Adams's declaration that "there may be exceptions" set the stage for a series of violent confrontations. In the early days of 1770, shopkeepers and merchants who showed any inclination to import found their windows broken, their signs defaced, and their images hung in effigy.

On 22 February a crowd of several hundred appeared before the shop of Theophilus Lillie, an alleged importer. As the mob prepared an effigy of poor Lillie, Ebenezer Richardson, a neighbor, stepped forward. Richardson, a notorious customs informer, soon found himself a target. He ran into his house and fired down on the crowd through a window, killing an 11-year-old German youth, Christopher Snider.

The young martyr's death sent the town into wild expressions of grief. Richardson barely escaped the rope while Snider's funeral drew a huge crowd. It was political brew of the best vintage, for it allowed the Sons to link a customs informer with the death of an "innocent" man. Snider's friends were eager for revenge.

CHAPTER 8

Massacre

❖
❖

While Adams railed at the treachery of weak-spirited merchants, he rejoiced that a notable foe, Francis Bernard, had fallen. After enduring one of the most torturous terms any royal governor had ever experienced, Bernard sailed for England with nary a regret. On 1 August he took leave at Long Wharf, and boarded HMS *Rippon* for the journey home. Not wanting to miss a chance to hurl a final dart, the *Gazette* commented on his departure: "embarked on board his Majesty's ship the *Rippon,* Sir Francis Bernard of Nettleham, Bart., who for nine Years past, has been a Scourge to this Province, a Curse to North-America, and a Plague to the whole Empire." No doubt Bernard had reciprocal feelings about the leaders of Boston.

Officially, Sir Francis was on leave, although no one seriously thought he would ever return to Massachusetts. In his stead, the ministry appointed an acting governor, Lt. Gov. Thomas Hutchinson.

Despite Adams's propaganda Thomas Hutchinson was not the devil incarnate. He may have been ambitious, a tad greedy, and given to favoring his relatives, but these were traits of many eighteenth-century British politicians. That was his fatal flaw; notwithstanding his nativity, his heart and mind were English. He was more concerned with pleasing the aristocrats of London than the people of Boston.

No community in British North America was more self-conscious of its history than Boston, and no one in this community was more active in interpreting it than Hutchinson. One of the great tragedies of the August Stamp Act riots and the attack on his home was that important documents he had been collecting to write a history of the colony had been destroyed by the rabble. Hutchinson felt the loss deeply and he despised those who had so diminished his contribution.

Like all historians, to a greater or lesser extent, Hutchinson viewed historic events through the prism of his own biases. He understood the empire to be a vital entity of which Massachusetts was a small part. The province had no history or destiny separate from that of the empire. Those who had left England to settle in the colony were still Englishmen, bound for all time to king and Parliament. To deny or alter that relationship was to risk disorder within and attack from without. To lose the empire would be tantamount to devolution into a state of nature.

Hutchinson's fears reduced him to an accommodationist. It is clear from his letters that he often disagreed with decisions made in London. Sometimes he voiced his opposition; on other occasions he remained silent and glum; but in all instances he yielded to London. Even when he believed that actions in London threatened Boston's liberties, he obeyed.

Like most people deeply committed to an ideal, Hutchinson was incapable of understanding how others could disagree with him. Even though nearly a century and a half had passed since Boston's founding, loyalty to the mother country remained for him a constant. He could not fathom the effects of time and geography on the minds of his fellow citizens.

In contrast, Adams had a different understanding of history. Not a mere outpost of the empire, Boston was a community whose citizens were bound to one another and to the empire. But those ties would hold only as long as all parties faithfully performed their mutual responsibilities. Perhaps as early as the Stamp Act, but certainly by the time Hutchinson assumed the governorship, Samuel Adams had come to believe that a conspiracy was afoot to undermine the liberties of Americans. It was, in his perception, a conspiracy concocted by sinister men on both sides of the Atlantic, many of whom were in the direct employ of the king.

All the reasons to seek independence, as cited so eloquently by Thomas Jefferson in the Declaration of Independence, were in place by 1770. Was Adams in favor of independence in 1770? Probably not. Even he still professed allegiance to the king, although not to Parliament. To Adams, the person of the king, albeit tarnished, still embodied the fundamental rights of Englishmen. To remain viable, however, symbols need to be constantly reinvented and reinvigorated. Hutchinson and his friends, instead of working to cultivate a new generation's loyalty to the mother country, seemed determined for their own selfish reasons to alienate the two parties. On a cold wintry night in March 1770, Bostonians saw just how distant the relationship had become.

Even by New England standards, the winter of 1769–1770 was harsh. By early March, a time when Bostonians usually began their wistful search for spring, the streets were still covered with a foot of packed, dirty snow. In front of the townhouse at the head of King Street, the snow had been even more compressed by the tramping feet of people doing business at the House, worshiping at the First Church only a few yards away, or even visiting across the street at the customhouse. This was the busiest crossroad in Boston where King, Queen, and Cornhill Streets converged at the Town House.

On the evening of 5 March 1770, however, the square was nearly empty. The moon in its first quarter shone down brightly, reflecting off the snow and ice. Near the customhouse stood a lone sentry, Private Hugh White. Most of the time he huddled inside the sentry house, but knowing his sergeant was about, every once and a while he marched forward, spent a few minutes in the open, and then returned to the shelter of the house.

White was a soldier of the Twenty-ninth Regiment, one of the four stationed in the town. He hated Boston. Name-calling, an occasional snowball tossed at him, and the constant lies printed in the *Journal,* all worked to make White and his comrades wish they were almost anywhere but Boston. Bostonians also wished the troops were somewhere else.

Sometime after eight o'clock that night a tall man in a white wig and red cloak was in seen in Dock Square. According to later testimony, the mysterious stranger warned a group of young men gathering round him that they best be on their guard. He swore that soldiers were roaming the streets with cudgels and cutlasses, looking to knock heads and slice off ears. The audience listened. Some went back to the tavern; others set out to find the soldiers.

Tories always accused Samuel Adams of being the mysterious provocateur. Adams, though, could hardly be described as tall. Still, when John Singleton Copley painted Adams, not long after the evening in question, he gave him red clothing. No matter the culprit, however, neither the soldiers nor the young Bostonians needed much encouragement to attack one another.

At the customhouse Hugh White worried when he saw a group of young men begin to congregate nearby. Snowballs arched toward him. He took his musket off his shoulder and brandished it, telling the boys to be gone. They taunted him, "Fire, and be damned." "The lobster dare not fire." Just then the bell in the First Church pealed. To those within earshot, who knew nothing of what was transpiring in front of the customhouse, the sound meant only one thing—fire. Dozens of people piled toward the square.

As they came toward the church, people heard and then saw the altercation between White and the boys. When White saw the crowd surging at him, he panicked. He sent a servant scurrying off for the remainder of the guard, who were quartered just up the street.

Capt. Thomas Preston, the officer in charge of the guard, was just finishing his supper. When he heard the commotion, he too came running. Preston and the remainder of the guard arrived at almost the same moment. With sword drawn, the captain pushed his way through the crowd, formed his men up in a semicircle, and called to the crowd to disperse. He also ordered his men to load, prime, and present their muskets. As the soldiers executed their order, one of them fell. As he went down, the hammer of his musket released. In an instant it discharged. The other soldiers, scared and confused, thought they were being attacked. They leveled their muskets and fired into the crowd.

When the smoke cleared on King Street, four men lay dead, another dragged himself off only to die, and six others were wounded. Not knowing what to expect, the soldiers loaded, primed, and leveled their muskets again. Meanwhile, drawn first by the noise of the bells and then the sound of gunfire, the governor rushed down from Province House. He later testified about the ugly scene he encountered. "Pressed by the people almost upon the Bayonets I called for the Officer. He came from between the Ranks." According to Hutchinson, he asked Captain Preston, "How come you to fire without Orders from a Civil Magistrate?" The officer's response was "imperfect." While Hutchinson was talking with the officer the crowd became even more agitated and pushed the governor and the guard toward the Town House. Hutchinson went inside with Captain Preston where the captain denied giving the order to fire.

Boston was in an uproar. The incident on King Street was quickly portrayed as "bloody butchery." The soldiers were arrested and held for trial. Paul Revere, with a keen eye for both profit and politics, rushed to publish an engraving of the "massacre." The visual message—smirking soldiers firing into a scampering crowd of Bostonians—was clear, but a few lines of patriotic doggerel were appended to the bottom of the engraving nonetheless.

Unhappy Boston! See thy Sons deplore,
Thy hallowed Walks besmeared with guiltless Gore.
While faithless P——n and his savage Bands
With murderous Rancour stretch their bloody Hands,

> Like fierce Barbarians grimacing o'er their Prey,
> Approve the carnage and enjoy the Day.

Hutchinson's query to Preston, "How come you to fire without Orders from a Civil Magistrate?" drove to the mark. Since Preston had no such orders, his only tactic, and that of his men, was to claim self-defense. To urge that view upon a candid world, Preston's lawyers would have to convince a jury that the citizens of Boston were a violent rabble who had created a murderous climate in their town. Convicting a town was likely to prove more difficult than finding eight redcoats and their captain guilty of murder.

To Adams the guilt or innocence of the accused soldiers was of minor importance. The trial provided Bostonians an opportunity to take the stage and show the world how vilely they had been abused by the empire's butchers. This was not a theoretical debate over natural rights or the authority of Parliament. This was about men being murdered. The shots on King Street had done more than shatter the bodies of five unlucky Bostonians; they had torn through the fabric connecting town and mother country. In Adams's view, any power that could send soldiers to do such work was a power that had abdicated its right to rule.

Even as the echoes of musketry died away, Adams, Hancock, and other town leaders gathered to lay plans. They agreed that the soldiers had to be ordered from the streets of Boston. The next morning, a delegation met with Hutchinson to make their demand. His reply was quite unsatisfactory. He informed his visitors that the troops were not under his command; the order to leave town would have to come from their commander, Col. William Dalrymple.

Thus dismissed, the delegation walked over to Faneuil Hall, where the rest of the town gathered. After a short prayer by the Reverend Cooper, Adams rose to speak. His grandson later wrote that Adams spoke on this occasion, as he was wont, with "nervous, impressive energy." Genuinely shocked as they were at what had happened on King Street, Bostonians listened attentively. Not a single dissent was heard when the

meeting voted to demand that the troops be removed to prevent further bloodshed. The meeting appointed a delegation of
15, headed by Adams, to present their demand to the governor.

Adams did not mince words with the governor. If the
troops were not removed, Bostonians would summon aid
from the nearby towns and together they would drive the redcoats into the sea. Hutchinson was told that "all the blood"
would be on his head alone. Taken aback, the governor feared
that he faced nothing less than a "general insurrection."

As chief actors in this high drama, both Hutchinson and
Adams well understood what was at stake—nothing less than
the future of British authority in Boston. Hutchinson was convinced that what had taken place on King Street was part of a
plot "of wicked and designing men." Among those men, the
governor thought, was Samuel Adams.

Did Samuel Adams and others plot the massacre? The
surviving documents neither confirm nor deny Hutchinson's
suspicions.

Perhaps no evidence ever existed, or perhaps descendants
of the participants destroyed it. We can never be certain. From
what is known of the people and events surrounding 5 March,
however, it does seem reasonable to suggest that coincidence
is a less than sufficient explanation.

Without question Bostonians engaged in a concerted effort
to harass the troops. Adams endorsed these efforts and well
understood that if the soldiers could be pushed into an outrageous act, it would rally the town. At a moment when nonimportation was faltering, Adams needed to resuscitate the patriot cause. For Hutchinson and Dalrymple in particular, the
overriding challenge was to maintain discipline among the
restless troops. Long bearing abuse from the citizens of Boston,
not trained to handle civil disorder, their nerves frazzled, they
would not take kindly to requests for patience.

Certain that he faced a conspiracy, Hutchinson initially refused to yield. Despite the pleas of those around him, including his brother-in-law, the governor hesitated to consult the
colonel. Should the people rise up though, Dalrymple's regi-

ments would be overwhelmed. He had just enough troops to anger Bostonians but not enough to stop them. Yapping spineless councilors, threats of more violence, and the realization that he would not be the victor in an armed confrontation convinced Hutchinson to swallow his pride and admit failure. When asked if he would remove the troops, Dalrymple quickly agreed.

But the colonel wanted a guarantee of safe conduct. He had two regiments in Boston: the Fourteenth and the notorious Twenty-ninth. The Twenty-ninth was quartered on the west side of the town and would have to march right through the heart of Boston.

Adams playfully recognized that Dalrymple's request was a perfect occasion to heap further humiliation on His Majesty's government while at the same time demonstrating Bostonians' gracious civility. On 10 March the Fourteenth proceeded quickly to their boats and rowed over to Castle William without incident. With a young drummer tapping out a quick step, the offensive Twenty-ninth Regiment, mostly Irishmen, marched briskly toward Wheelwrights Wharf. As Dalrymple had requested, the town sent an escort to protect the soldiers—one man—Will Molineux, who strode beside the troops unarmed. It was a curious and, for the soldiers, a shameful spectacle. Regiments of His Majesty's army, an army that had amassed an empire, were now being protected by a single man.

Adams and his cohorts did not hold sway in every matter. They had wanted a quick trial for the soldiers to maintain the town at its pitch. Hutchinson wanted time to cool passions. Prevailing in this instance, the governor managed to delay the trials of Preston and the soldiers until the fall.

In the months leading to the trial, Adams worked tirelessly to spread news of the horrid event throughout America and overseas to England. It was critical that Boston be seen as a martyr. Central to Adams's strategy was the necessity for a "fair trial," which required securing good counsel for Preston and his men. There could be none better than John Adams and Josiah Quincy.

Unfortunately we will never know what ultimately persuaded John Adams and Josiah Quincy to take on such a thoroughly unpopular task. To the dismay of historians, one of the few significant gaps in John Adams's otherwise comprehensive diary occurs between February and June 1770. According to a recollection written more than 30 years after the event, Adams received a visit from a friend of Preston's. The caller tearfully implored Adams to represent the captain and his soldiers. Rising to the challenge, Adams vehemently declared that this was a "free Country" and everyone "ought to have the Council they preferred." "Without hesitation," he offered his services.

John Adams was an honorable and honest man, but his recollection seems a bit self-serving, especially when compared with Josiah Quincy's account. In a letter to his father, written less than three weeks after the massacre, Quincy made it abundantly clear that he was deeply concerned about how Boston would view him if he defended the British. Indeed, when first asked to serve as counsel, he refused. Only after he had been "advised and urged to undertake it, by an Adams, a Hancock, a Molineux, a Cushing, a Henshaw, a Pemberton, a Warren, a Cooper, and a Phillips" did he consent to represent the soldiers. Quincy need not have fretted, for by serving the soldiers he served the town.

Adams and Quincy had ample time to prepare a defense. Through the summer, as temperatures rose, passions cooled just as Hutchinson had hoped. Adams did everything he could to keep the political pot boiling. As "A Chatterer," "A Tory," and "Vindex," he filled Edes and Gill's *Gazette* with articles intended to deepen distrust of royal authority. Almost as if by choice, the king's officers made his job easier. Hutchinson, for example, aroused suspicions of a sinister transatlantic plot by refusing to make public any communication from the ministry. When the General Court assembled in September, the governor, at the order of the ministry, forced the body to meet in Cambridge at Harvard College, away from their usual place of business in Boston.

Through the pages of the *Gazette,* Adams raised the specter of conspiracy between the governor and his minions on this side of the Atlantic and the ministry's toadies on the other. Presiding over these machinations was the king. Attacking the sovereign, however, had always been out of bounds. Whatever evil befell the colonies was not the responsibility of the king but of those who served him ill. By keeping the sovereign beyond reproach the personage of the king remained a continuing bond for all in the empire.

In "Chatterer," however, Adams moved perilously close to assailing the person of the king, the very symbol of empire. The king was perhaps no better, and maybe even worse, than those who served him. For the moment, Adams merely teased out a possibility. While he might be willing to unmask the king as a corrupt tyrant, those around him were ill prepared for such heresy. If the king was demystified and made to appear as venal as his ministers, nothing would be left to bind the empire.

On Wednesday, 24 October 1770, at 8 A.M., the trials finally got underway. Preston, tried separately from his men, was first on the docket. The prosecution may have sensed its danger as early as jury selection. With adroitness Quincy and Adams managed to secure a jury on which not a single Bostonian sat.

By eighteenth-century standards the trial was long—five days. Preston's cause was aided immeasurably by the incompetency of the prosecution, which Andrew Oliver dubbed "unfit." Of course, if they had been "fit," and won the case, Captain Preston would have gone to the gibbet on Boston Common. Such a solemn sight would have embarrassed the royal government and tagged Boston as a vengeful community. Convicting Preston did not serve the interests of either side. He was acquitted.

With Preston acquitted, the soldiers, whose trial opened on 27 November, could not claim they were simply following orders. Their best defense was to prove that their lives had been threatened by the townsmen and they had acted in self-defense. This was precisely what Samuel Adams had anticipated and it was for this reason that he had urged Quincy and

Adams to defend the soldiers. He knew he could count on his patriotic friends to use restraint, to muster only that evidence necessary to gain acquittal. The town's reputation would be safe. Samuel was not disappointed. Thanks to the incompetence of the crown, the same incompetence that had helped win Preston's acquittal, Adams and Quincy were able to suppress evidence that might have embarrassed the town.

It took the jury less than three hours to reach a verdict. Of the eight soldiers charged, six were acquitted and set free. Two, Hugh Montgomery and Matthew Killroy, were convicted of manslaughter. They "prayed clergy," a medieval custom that allowed them to escape a death sentence. Instead they were branded on the thumb so they might never again offer such a plea.

Samuel Adams's propagandistic use of the event did not end with the sentencing. According to Vindex, the "blood thirsty" butchers on King Street had done their work with "Savage barbarity" and should have received condign punishment. In article after article, Adams, with scant regard for the truth, railed at the horrid injustice of letting the massacre perpetrators go free. For anyone who had heard about the events on King Street, Vindex was hardly an objective source. But Adams was not addressing Boston. His propaganda aimed at the less well informed who were far beyond the confines of the town, those who could be persuaded that Boston's situation was truly pitiable.

Adams did his best to keep hate alive, which was not easy. Signs that tensions were easing were everywhere. In December the commissioners of the customs quietly returned from their self-imposed exile at Castle William and held their meetings in the town with "no complaints of Insults or any sort of Molestation." Their image had been much improved the previous April when the Townshend duties, save the one on tea, had been repealed. The regiments whose presence had done so much to stir crisis were no longer in the town. The Fourteenth remained quartered at the castle and the infamous Twenty-ninth was on duty in New Jersey.

John Rowe, one of Adams's vacillating merchant allies who rejoiced at the trial's outcome, cared little for the guilt or innocence of the soldiers; he only wanted the town to get beyond this ugliness to a renewal of "Harmony Peace & Friendship." Hutchinson even boasted to a friend "that I have succeeded beyond what the friends of Government expected and that it is now the sense of a great part, perhaps the majority of the people of the Province, Boston excepted, that the late measures [i.e., street protests] are not to be justified."

Hutchinson mistook a temporary calm for a full abatement of the storm; nonetheless, his self-serving comments had some foundation. With the repeal of the Townshend duties, nonimportation was collapsing. While there was little that he could do to reclaim the pusillanimous merchants of New York, Philadelphia, Charleston, and the other ports, in Boston, at least, Adams was determined to hold the line. Boston merchants, though, saw no reason why they should impose suffering upon themselves while their colleagues in other ports reaped a harvest. Having sided with Adams and his friends earlier, albeit sometimes only after some serious arm-twisting, they now wanted to part company and resume business. Adams was not about to let them walk away. The postmassacre rapprochement made his task more difficult.

Words were not enough, so Adams and "his Faneuil Hall friends" once more turned to the time-honored mass meeting and threats of mob action. It was all too late, for the spirit of resistance driving nonimportation was dead. Adams had miscalculated. He thought the merchants would stay with him in defense of principle. He held the community to be one body standing united against the duties, the men who had enacted them, and the ill-conceived philosophy that had given them birth. In truth, the motives of the merchants were far more base. Profits, not philosophy, directed their actions.

It was a melancholy moment for Samuel Adams. Sadly he watched his town, like all of America, scramble over the crumbled wall of nonimportation. Adams hoped that the "edge of resentment" would not be dulled, but he held little faith that the merchants would help him keep it sharp. Henceforth, he proclaimed, he would rely on the "body of the people." Nor would he confine his efforts to Boston alone. All Americans, he insisted, "are resolved they *will not* be Slaves." Adams had come to understand that only by drawing together the force of the "body of people" everywhere could he overcome the cupidity of the merchants anywhere. Through the lens of experience, Adams gradually had come to focus on his enemies—a royal government and its minions supported by avaricious merchants on this side of the Atlantic, in league with a corrupt and venal ministry in London, abetted in their designs by an ignorant, if not culpable monarch. Given this scenario, Adams can hardly have entertained any hopes of reconciliation.

CHAPTER 9

Tea and Intolerables

❖
❖

Samuel Adams was concerned. All around him he witnessed backsliding, complacency, and compromise. Boston's spirit of resistance, once vigorous, was faltering. In March came news that Hutchinson had been appointed governor, and his brother-in-law Andrew Oliver, lieutenant governor. Both their salaries were to be paid from the royal treasury, thereby making them independent of the Massachusetts House. Adams lambasted his old enemy as a "tyrant," "usurper," "malevolent," but it had little impact. For the time, at least, the native-born Hutchinson was popular, and his appointment was welcomed as a sign of reconciliation with London. Adams's depression grew deeper.

In a letter to his friend Arthur Lee in Virginia, he wrote, "there never was a time when the political Affairs of America were in a more dangerous State; Such is the Indolence of Men in general, or their Inattention to the real importance of things, that a steady & animated perseverance in the rugged path of Virtue at the hazard of trifles is hardly to be expected." People "engaged in private Business for the Support of their own families" found it hard to "agree on one consistent plan of Opposition while the appointed Instruments of Oppression, have all the Means of applying to the passions of

Men & availing themselves of the Necessity of some, the Vanity of others & the timidity of all." With so many in his own community having succumbed to passion, timidity, and vanity, Adams could little trust the wider community to tread the "rugged path of Virtue."

Adams truly saw himself as a virtuous man. Like Henry V's "band of brothers," he and a few others still stood together in a moment of history. Through the press, the House, and the town meeting, Adams fought to expose the evil masking itself as legitimate authority, while his fellow citizens were drawn from the defense of their liberties by the blandishments of a vice-ridden royal government. Nonetheless, Adams held to his faith that in time, and with just cause, his countrymen would return to their principles and embrace the covenant that for more than six generations had been their spiritual strength.

Adams matched his faith with works. He saw to it, for example, that every 5 March the town was reminded of the awful events on King Street. The 1771 commemoration set a model followed for many years. At noon the bells began to peal, and for one hour they tolled remembrance. In the evening, a "true son of liberty," Dr. Thomas Young, who had moved from Albany to Boston in 1766, delivered the Massacre Day oration. With sadness, Young recounted the events of 5 March and reminded his audience of how bravely the people of Massachusetts had defied the "minions of the throne."

At the conclusion of the speech, the crowd moved toward the home of Paul Revere, where they were treated to tableaux. One depicted the "ghost of Christopher Snider, with one of his fingers in the wound, endeavoring to stop the blood issuing therefrom." Another "represented the soldiers drawn up, firing at the people assembled before them,—the dead on the ground, and the wounded falling, with blood running in streams from their wounds." The third and final sanguinary tableau displayed "the figure of a woman, representing AMERICA, sitting on the stump of a tree, with a staff in her hand, and the cap of liberty on the top thereof; one foot on the head of a grenadier, lying prostrate, grasping a serpent."

Staged for the common folk—the people who did not read
Edes and Gill and who paid little note to metaphysical arguments over "natural rights" or the "British constitution"—the
tableaux, like the emotional orator, were an effective propaganda device. But they could reach only those present at their
performance. Beyond the town, Tory propagandists were suc-
cessfully portraying Adams and the Boston Sons as violent,
mobbish men who would not be satisfied until Massachusetts
was "totally democratical." Such images played well with the
folks in the countryside who had always viewed the port as a
sinkhole of iniquity.

For a time the Tories seemed to have things progressing in
their favor. Boston was calm; London was silent; and the
troops were gone. Many believed that peace, harmony, and
prosperity had once more been achieved. Hutchinson was not
so sure. He had hoped the optimists were right, but he was realist enough to recognize that as long as Samuel Adams drew
breath, nothing could be taken for granted. He wrote to London of his foe, "I doubt whether there is a greater Incendiary in
the King's dominions or a man of greater malignity of heart, or
who less scruples any measure ever so criminal to accomplish
his purposes; and I think I do him no injustice when I suppose
he wishes the destruction of every Friend to Government in
America."

The great "Incendiary" had trouble kindling the fire.
Adams lamented that his townsmen had been seduced by the
governor and his minions. With promises of preferment,
Hutchinson had crafted a following. Even Adams's erstwhile
ally John Hancock seemed lured by Hutchinson's siren song.
Not altogether happy with Adams's leadership, Hancock
found him contentious, uncompromising, and overbearing. It
was not long before Hutchinson learned of Hancock's sim-
mering disaffection. Sensing there might be a chance for
advantage, Hutchinson signaled to Hancock that "upon a
change of sentiments everything past would be entirely forgotten, and it would be a pleasure to the governor to consent
to his election to the council." Not only was Hancock elected

to the council in 1772, but he was also appointed colonel of cadets by His Excellency.

Distressed, but not defeated, Puritan Adams laid plans for a counterattack. Although at heart somber and serious, Adams was also the consummate optimist. He believed that when properly informed, most people, aside from unregenerate ministerial toadies, would try to do the "right thing," that is, what he thought they should. Properly informing people was a matter of education and communication: finding the truth and sharing it with others. Adams had done precisely that when as clerk of the House he had sent letters to correspondents in London and the other colonies. He had done the same through the pages of the *Gazette* in the personae of Candidus and Vindex.

Adams shared his concerns with Arthur Lee of Virginia. He asked Lee if "Societies should be formed" whose members might "correspond" with each other. "And if conducted with a proper spirit, would it not afford reason for the Enemies of our common Liberty, however great, to tremble." It was, admitted Adams, "a sudden Thought & drops undigested from my pen. It would be an arduous Task for any man to attempt to awaken a sufficient Number in the Colonies to so grand an Undertaking. Nothing however should be despaired of."

As Adams thought more on the subject his depression lifted. It would indeed be an "arduous Task" to fashion new societies, but Massachusetts had its own "societies"—battle tested ready to respond and tied together in an elaborate and encompassing network. Adams had already relied upon this network—the colony's town meetings—to spread his message. With the help of Thomas Young, he laid his new plan.

First, Adams and Young hit upon using the designation *Committee of Correspondence.* By adopting a term widely recognized by all the colonial assemblies, they avoided any appearance of innovation or radicalism that might taint their message and alert opponents to their aims. To further disguise his goal, Adams was willing to let Young take the greater role in organizing the effort. Young relished the chance, and in high spirits he wrote to a friend, "we are brewing something here which will make some people's heads reel." Yet Young also understood that plans carefully laid were more apt to succeed than those hastily thrown together. Preparing the way he and Adams moved slowly but surely.

The conspirators knew that Boston could never stand alone, nor could it be perceived as espousing any cause for solely its own benefit. Any grievance discussed must be shared by all the towns. As usual a bumbling ministry handed the patriots the grievance round which they could rally.

Late in 1771, when the ministry had announced that henceforth the governor would be paid off the civil list, that is, his salary would come from the king and not the General Court, there had been mutterings in the town. Nonetheless, there was ample precedent for such a policy, and while Bostonians might persist in their annoyance, the issue had little staying power. Judges, however, were a different matter. Since the Act of Settlement of 1701, judges were held to be constitutionally independent. In England independence was generally achieved through judicial tenure whereby justices held their commissions for life, with no restrictions, save for "good behavior." In the colonies the situation was more delicate. Judges could be removed by the governor with little or no cause. On the other hand, the General Court paid judges' salaries. In a crude way the arrangement had fostered a certain balance of power between the government and the people. It had also made it difficult for the king's officers to enforce unpopular laws.

In the early fall of 1772 came news of the sort for which Adams and Young had been yearning. Judges of the Superior Court would henceforth, like the governor, be paid off the civil list. Here was an issue that struck at all. Writing as "Valerius Poplicola," Adams asked,

> Is it not enough, to have a Governor, an avowed Advocate for ministerial Measures, and a most assiduous Instrument in carrying them on—model'd, shaped, controul'd, and directed—totally independent of the people over whom he is commissioned to govern, and yet absolutely dependent

> upon the Crown paid out of a Revenue establish'd by those
> who have no Authority to establish it, and extorted from the
> People in a Manner most Odious, insulting and oppressive.

In addition, "the iron Hand of Tyranny" threatened to place "the murderous Rage of lawless Power on the sacred Seat of Justice." Adams called on "every Town [to] assemble. Let Associations & Combinations be everywhere set up to consult and recover our just Rights."

Adams, Young, and the Boston Whigs answered their own call. By mid-October a petition was circulated asking for a special town meeting to discuss the most recent attack on the people's liberties.

On 28 October, with Hancock sitting as moderator, a special meeting convened with only one item on the warrant. "A vast majority" of the meeting approved a resolution conveying Boston's grave concern and asking what information His Excellency could offer in the matter. A committee of five, led by Adams, was elected to deliver the inquiry.

The governor was not in a mood to cooperate. His correspondence with his superiors in London was confidential. Bluntly and without ceremony, he told the delegation that he had no intention of sharing it with them. On 30 October the town's special meeting reconvened to receive the governor's reply. Not satisfied with what they heard, they petitioned Hutchinson to convene the General Court. He rejected the request. Then, not realizing how neatly he played into Adams's hands, he explained himself. He pointed out that town meetings had only limited authority and were not entitled to discuss matters beyond those relating to local governance. It was then clear the issue of the moment was no business of town meeting.

Adams cannot have wanted more. In one fell swoop Hutchinson assaulted publicly two sacred institutions, town meeting and the General Court—the twin pillars of representative government. Adams relished the opportunity that Hutchinson had presented him, but he also appreciated the need for caution. Boston's response must not be too dramatic or too radical, lest the other towns be scared off. The goal was to bring the other towns "to reason, and make them our friends." At the meeting of 2 November, Adams offered a resolution:

> That a Committee of Correspondence be appointed to state the Rights of the Colonists and of this Province in particular, as Men, as Christians, and as Subjects; to communicate and publish the same to the several Towns in this Province and to the World as the sense of this Town, with the Infringements and Violations thereof that have been, or from time to time may be made—Also requesting of each Town a free communication of their Sentiments on this Subject.

On 20 November 1772 the resolution passed unanimously. Immediately a subcommittee consisting of Samuel Adams, James Otis, and Josiah Quincy prepared a declaration of "The Rights of the Colonists." The draft was in the hand of Samuel Adams.

Anticipating Thomas Jefferson's Declaration four years hence, the address began with a philosophy of government and an articulation of rights. Then followed a lengthy chronicle of how those rights had been violated. The document was intentionally long, legalistic, and laborious. Adams was a master of rhetoric and could have written otherwise, but he matched his style to his purpose, which was to present the issues in as clinical a fashion as possible. Those who took the trouble to wade through the rhetoric would be captivated by its dispassionate, inescapable logic, a logic that wrapped itself around all the communities of Massachusetts.

James Warren of Plymouth, Elbridge Gerry of Marblehead, Joseph Hawley of Northampton, and Joseph Otis of Barnstable, all warm Whigs, read "The Rights of the Colonists" and wrote Adams, offering their support and promising to urge their towns to stand with Boston. From the vast majority of towns, however, the response was silence. To his radical friends, Adams counseled patience. He had faith that with persistence and time, the somnolent towns would awaken.

Thomas Hutchinson did his unwitting best to stir the towns. He could not let the ideas circulated by the Boston committee go unchallenged. They were, in his mind, seditious.

"He threw all caution to the wind, [and] summoned the Assembly together for an emergency session." The body convened on 6 January to attend to His Excellency.

Hutchinson apologized for troubling the assemblymen, but he insisted the crisis demanded it. He spoke not only as their governor but also as their historian. His message was clear: From its very beginnings the province of Massachusetts Bay was "subject to the supreme authority of Parliament." While Massachusetts and the other colonies were granted their own assemblies, these bodies had always been, and must continue to be, "subordinate" to Parliament. Driving to his point, Hutchinson declared before his rapt audience, "I know of no line that can be drawn between the supreme authority of Parliament and the total independence of the colonies." For once, Samuel Adams was in full agreement. Their agreement on principle, however, would lead to very different conclusions.

Hutchinson's combative response, along with the "Rights of the Colonists" was printed and distributed throughout the colonies. Here, for the first time, in language clear and contradictory, readers could take measure of the two opposing sides. That Hutchinsion could not see how his position would be manipulated is indicative of his competence as a historian. He may well have been a master at collecting facts, but he was woefully inept at interpreting them. Where Adams saw the evolution and empowerment of his community, Hutchinson saw a continuous and unchanging relationship whereby the colonies were and would always be subservient to Parliament. This was not a matter subject to rigorous intellectual examination; it involved how people felt about their history and their community. As the people of Sudbury, Massachusetts, had said more than a century before, "We shall be judged by people of our own choosing." No matter what Hutchinson argued, members of Parliament were not of the colonists' choosing.

Samuel Adams helped make Thomas Hutchinson a miserable man. Adams happily watched his old adversary slowly sink in popular esteem. He wished that the old deacon had lived to see his enemy embarrassed. In June 1773 a packet of letters arrived from London designated for the speaker of the House. They had been dispatched by Benjamin Franklin, the Massachusetts agent in London. Altogether there were 13 letters in the packet, written by Thomas Hutchinson and four of his friends and relatives, including his brother-in-law Andrew Oliver. Most of the letters were addressed to Thomas Whately, a late member of Parliament and influential cabinet minister.

On 2 June 1773 these letters were read to a closed session of the House. Two weeks later, they were published in a pamphlet which, on the title page, promised that within the reader would find "the fatal source of the confusion and bloodshed in which this province especially has been involved and which threatened total destruction to the liberties of all *America.*" The language had the unmistakable ring of Samuel Adams.

The letters failed to fulfill their promise, for they disclosed little that Hutchinson had not divulged elsewhere. He observed that "a colony 3000 miles distant from the parent state" could not "enjoy all the liberty of the parent state," but his call for "an abridgment of what are called English liberties" in the colonies was intolerable. These letters, bundled together with the untoward policies of Parliament over the last decade, bolstered the Whig claim that a conspiracy was afoot to destroy the liberties of the people. By his own hand, Thomas Hutchinson had given evidence of his and the ministry's evil intent. In the eyes of Samuel Adams, the governor's crime was quadrupled by the fact that he was a Bostonian, not a London toady sent by the ministry. He had, in fact, betrayed his own community.

By way of the Boston Committee of Correspondence, copies of the pamphlet revealing the conspiracy among "evil Men in this Province" were distributed to all the towns. In the House, Adams presented a petition to the king asking that Hutchinson and Lt. Gov. Oliver be recalled. It passed by a vote of 80 to 11. For his own peace of mind, Hutchinson had already made the painful decision to leave.

Had the king's ministers been wiser they might have moved more slowly. Given all that had happened in Massachusetts—riots, boycotts, controversies over judges' salaries, and now the humiliation of the governor—the king's ministers would have done well to ponder and pause to allow time for consolidation before moving forward. In retrospect, the ministry often seemed to have been in a mild frenzy to impose new policies on the colonies even as the old ones failed. The pace of change as much as the change itself sparked colonial opposition. Sir Frederick North, the prime minister, failed to grasp that principle. He disdained to allow the colonies any breathing space, and in the matter of tea saw an opportunity to raise revenue and make a political point. As he put it, "The properest time to exert our right of taxation is when the right is refused. The properest time for making resistance is when we are attacked." On 10 May 1773 Parliament passed the Tea Act of 1773.

North wove a complex scheme designed to accomplish three goals: provide a profit for the East India Company, raise a revenue, and reinforce Parliament's right to tax the colonies. The act granted the company a drawback on English duties and allowed them to ship tea directly to the colonies, where it was consigned to specific merchants for sale. The tea carried a tax of 3d per pound. By North's calculations, East India tea, despite the tax, would still sell at a price less than the smuggled Dutch variety. On 18 October the tea ships *Eleanor, Dartmouth, Beaver,* and *William* caught a fair breeze at Deal and set off for Boston.

News of the Tea Act had been ill received throughout America. The outcry was particularly clamorous in New York and Philadelphia, where in early October citizens voted to consider an "enemy" anyone who aided in the sale of the detested tea. In both Philadelphia and New York the local Sons of Liberty demanded that the tea consignees resign or face the prospect of tarring and feathering. Even in the South, consignees were forced to withdraw. While the Sons triumphed in the rest of America, in Boston they stumbled as they ran into obstacles deriving from family loyalties and a stubborn governor.

Boston's tea consignees were three in number—the firms of Thomas and Elisha Hutchinson; Richard Clarke and Sons, and Faneuil and Winslow. Thomas and Elisha were sons of the governor. Richard Clarke's daughter was married to the younger Thomas Hutchinson. Faneuil and Winslow would follow the other two firms. With the governor at their side, the Hutchinson boys, Clarke, and Faneuil and Winslow all refused to yield.

By refusing to resign, the consignees embarrassed Boston. Knowing they had the governor's support, the tea consignees ignored a summons to the Liberty Tree. Given its dramatic history, Boston's failure to lead the way in the tea crisis was a matter of some note in the rest of America. From Philadelphia, for example, came the charge, "There are many fears respecting Boston, some even going to the length of asserting that tea was being imported and the duty paid." Similar unkind observations drifted up from New York City.

The situation in which Boston found itself was immensely distressing for Adams. Under heavy pressure from the Sons and the public in general, the consignees finally agreed to resign but only if the tea was landed and put under the care of the governor. That proposal was unacceptable, since everyone knew that once the tea went ashore it would, one way or another, be sold and the tax paid. Adams was determined not to see the tea landed.

On 28 November *Dartmouth* arrived. She dropped anchor in King's Roads, about three miles out from the town. Within a few days *Eleanor* and *Beaver* joined her. To ensure no tea was surreptitiously landed, the town insisted that the vessels leave their anchorage and make fast along Griffin's Wharf, where the Boston Committee of Correspondence posted a guard.

By law, the duty on the tea had to be paid within 20 days— by 17 December—otherwise the customs officers would move to seize it and then proceed to public auction. On the day after *Dartmouth*'s arrival, a mass meeting was held in Faneuil Hall. So many filed in that the meeting had to be adjourned to the Old South, where, by unanimous vote, resolutions demanded that the tea be sent back to England.

Adams saw to it that Boston would not stand alone. He called on the Committees of Correspondence from Charlestown,

Cambridge, Brookline, Roxbury, and Dorchester for advice and asked that they "be in readiness to exert themselves in the most resolute manner to assist this Town in their efforts for saving this oppressed Country." Those towns and others responded with resolutions of support. The special town meeting assembled again at the Old South on 14 December. Once more it demanded that the customs officers allow the tea to leave Boston and be returned to England without paying the duty; once more the request was denied. On the sixteenth, during yet another meeting at the Old South, the assembly sent a messenger to ask the governor to grant leave for the ships to withdraw. He refused. Having exhausted all their peaceful options, the meeting turned to Adams, who by this time was standing in the pulpit high above the crowd. He declared to them, "this meeting can do nothing further to save the country." With that remark, "Mohawk" Indians appeared in the aisles beckoning the crowd down to the harbor to see how well tea and saltwater mixed.

The crowd swirled down to Griffin's Wharf, marching behind the whooping "Mohawks." They boarded the three vessels and over the next few hours more than 10,000 pounds of tea were dumped into Boston harbor. The "Mohawks" were careful not to destroy any property save the tea. No one was injured. Having finished their work the "Mohawks" and the crowd dispersed into the night leaving windrows of tea to wash up on the shores of Boston Harbor.

If Adams went to the Tea Party he never admitted he had done so. He wasted no time, however, publicizing it. First he rallied the Committee of Correspondence to ensure that the word spread among the towns and beyond without delay. Next he wrote to his personal correspondents, one of the most important being Arthur Lee Adams's Virginia friend. After describing the events leading to the Tea Party and the party itself, Adams went on to tell Lee, "You cannot imagine the height of joy that sparkles in the eyes and animates the countenances as well as the hearts of all we meet on this occasion; excepting the disappointed, disconcerted Hutchinson and his tools."

As distressed as Hutchinson and his "tools" were, the ministers in London were even more agitated. To them Boston was a symbol of defiant lawlessness. For more than a decade, the people of Boston had protested, defied, and rioted against lawful authority. To allow them to go unpunished for this latest outrage was only to invite shame on His Majesty's government and foster the spread of sedition. Lord North decided to punish the town, chastise its citizens, and take measures to guarantee that such actions never happened again. Some extremists in the ministry urged cutting off the head of the serpent "send over Adams, Molineux, and other principal incendiaries, try them, and if found guilty, put them to death." Not even Lord North's pique reached those heights; nonetheless, he was determined to take harsh measures.

In the spring of 1774 the ministry revealed just how harsh it could be with the issuance of the Coercive Acts. They were indeed punitive. Even the beleaguered Thomas Hutchinson was taken aback at their severity.

First to pass Parliament in late March was the Boston Port Bill. Declaring that Boston was no longer a safe place to conduct commerce, the legislation closed the port until His Majesty was satisfied that the citizens of the town had made full restitution for the tea they had destroyed. Moreover, since Boston was unfit for commerce, it was also unsuitable for government, and so the House would remove to Salem. In parliamentary debates North made it clear that more measures would follow. Indeed, the spirit of revenge was so warm that one member cried out, "Delenda est Cathago."[1]

True to his threat, in April North engineered three more bills through Parliament. The Administration of Justice Act stipulated that the governor could send home for trial all

---

[1]This is a reference to Marcus Porcius Cato, the Roman statesman. Rome and Carthage were at war and Cato so hated Carthage that he cried out in the Senate, "Delenda est Cathago" meaning "Carthage must be destroyed."

crown officers accused of committing crimes in the conduct of their duties—a measure Adams hyperbolically referred to as the "Murderers's Act."

The Quartering Act permitted the commander in chief of the king's forces in America to seize barns and other unoccupied structures to board troops. Had this law been in effect earlier, the redcoats might have been in the center of Boston rather than isolated out at Castle William.

By far the most pernicious of the Coercive Acts was the Massachusetts Government Act. It struck at the heart of what Samuel Adams and his fellow citizens held most dear—their local government. The act dictated that henceforth council members would be appointed by the king and no longer be elected by the House. Juries would be impaneled by sheriffs appointed directly by the governor, who would also have the authority to appoint judges of the inferior court of common pleas. As arbitrary and obnoxious as those changes were to the people of Massachusetts, they paled in comparison to the assault on town meeting.

Town meeting was the heart and soul of the community. Again and again that remarkable institution had demonstrated its ability to rise and resist any invasion of the people's liberties. It could meet quickly and remain in session at will. It symbolized autonomy and community. It was, Lord North seems to have understood, the enemy of Parliament. Now, by decree, town meetings were to convene only once in a year, and their agendas could not stray beyond the bounds of electing town officers and enacting local ordinances.

Lord North may not have been a foolish man, but he was certainly mistaken. In focusing punishment on Boston, he believed he had avoided the error of his predecessors. Grenville, Townshend, and the others had supported measures touching all Americans, and had thereby raised the general ire. North set his sights on Boston and expected that other Americans, unaffected by the Coercive Acts, would ignore the plight of the Yankee town. What North had failed to gauge was the degree of intercolonial association, developed through such devices as the Committees of Correspondence. He had also failed to fully calculate the skill of Samuel Adams and others to use those avenues to persuade their fellow Americans that the frontier of American liberty lay on the banks of the Charles River. This argument held that Boston's tragedy was simply the opening act for a drama that would soon encompass all the colonies.

Sentiments of support flooded into Boston. On behalf of the people of Connecticut, Silas Deane wrote Adams that Boston was "suffering in the common cause." From Virginia came news that Burgesses had set 1 June (the day on which the port of Boston was to be closed) as "a day of fasting, humiliation, and prayer; devoutly to implore the divine interposition, for averting the heavy calamity which threatens destruction to our civil rights, and the evils of civil war; to give us one heart and one mind firmly to oppose, by all just and proper means, every injury to American rights." From Rhode Island, New York, and Philadelphia similarly sympathetic messages arrived. People from all the colonies were speaking with one voice and that voice was unmistakably "American."

Also received were calls for a general congress. Adams was skeptical. He wanted more immediate and direct action. He urged the approval of a "Solemn League and Covenant," a new and stricter variation of nonimportation. When the Boston Committee of Correspondence endorsed that option, the merchants, recognizing they had been deliberately bypassed, complained the committee had exceeded its authority.

Boston's merchants were not alone in their reluctance to accept Adams's radical position. Conservative forces scrambled to find an alternative to derail Adams's plan. Their answer was to call a congress, hoping that talk would replace action. Gradually through the spring and into the summer, the colonial legislatures signaled their agreement to send delegates to a meeting in Philadelphia. Adams was not particularly pleased at the prospect of more debate. It was, however, a price he would willingly pay if the discussion was to lead toward unity.

CHAPTER 10

The First Continental Congress

❖
❖

In the midst of Boston's troubles a new governor was installed. After a pleasant spring passage of less than four weeks, Gen. Thomas Gage arrived in Boston on 13 May 1774. He landed first at Castle William where he found Hutchinson disconsolate. The soon-to-be displaced governor had taken up residence in the fort to avoid the insults of the Boston mob. For four days the old and new governors were closeted together in somber discussion. Hutchinson was weary and bitter. For years he had borne the brunt of the province's refractory politics, and now he was pleased to unload that burden on Gage as he described to him the politics and personalities of the patriot machine.

Gage listened politely. The general was no stranger to America. He had served as an officer during the French and Indian War and for nearly a decade he had been His Majesty's commander in chief in the colonies. His wife, Margaret Kemble, was an American born in New Jersey. Indeed, Gage understood Massachusetts so well that it was only with great reluctance he had accepted the post as governor, and even then he demanded and received far more power than his predecessors had enjoyed.

On 17 May General Gage's barge pulled away from the castle and made its way up the harbor to Long Wharf. Thousands gathered near the wharf and watched as the governor and his party processed up King Street to the State House. All seemed calm, but the next evening, at a dinner in Faneuil Hall, Gage got his first inkling of the town's temper. When a councilor offered a toast to Governor Hutchinson, he was greeted with a loud and general hiss.

On 25 May Gage got another troubling political message when the new House sent to him the names of 18 new councilors. A quick glance down the list told him that most of the men were enemies of the government. The next day he dismissed 13 of them and then ordered the House to recess and in accordance with the Port Bill, reconvened in Salem.

Thomas Hutchinson held to a devil theory on Massachusetts politics. In his view, all could be well in the colony if a few radical troublemakers, most prominently Samuel Adams, were simply silenced or removed. He blamed a small coterie of evil men for making his life miserable and stirring the people to resistance. That view by 1774 was hopelessly and clearly wrong. Thomas Hutchinson had lived through a decade of turmoil and had learned almost nothing from the experience.

Gage understood that Adams, Hancock, and the others commanded a movement that had broad popular support. It had taken Adams more than a decade to muster that support, but by the summer of 1774, he basked in his success: A majority of the people of Boston, and perhaps of the colony at large, stood with Adams. General Gage faced a people edging toward rebellion.

If General Gage had any doubts about the cunning of his opponents, those questions were quickly resolved at the Salem meeting of the General Court. Early in the session, the House elected a committee to inquire into the state of the province. It was stacked with Whig members. One, Robert Treat Paine, recalled Adams's role in the committee. "Smooth & placid Observations [were] made by Mr. S. Adams, saying that it [the tea party including its aftermath] was an irritating affair & must be handled Cautiously."

Again employing a tried-and-true tactic, Adams and his friends waited to make their move until late in the session, when many of the members, loyalists among them, had already set out for home. On 17 June, the House ordered the public excluded from its deliberations; the entrance to the chamber was locked. The province secretary, who was carrying an order from the governor to dissolve the House, could not gain entry. With the secretary fuming outside, the House proceeded to pass a series of measures condemning the Port Act, recommending aid to relieve Boston, and, finally, electing Adams, Paine, James Bowdoin, Thomas Cushing, and John Adams as delegates to the Continental Congress scheduled to convene in Philadelphia in September.

Through its open defiance of the governor, the House had deeply embarrassed His Excellency and, even worse, shown him to be impotent. Over the next several weeks, General Gage's unhappy lot was to remain impassive as the countryside "worked up to a fury." Blatantly disregarding the Massachusetts Government Act, special town and county meetings assembled to pass fiery resolutions condemning Parliament's acts and urging resistance. Fearful for their safety, supporters of the governor and the king quietly packed their belongings and trudged across Boston Neck to seek protection behind red-coated sentries and the imposing guns of His Majesty's fleet.

As affairs tumbled forward, Adams prepared himself for Philadelphia. He consulted with his good friend Dr. Joseph Warren. Adams was concerned that while most of the other counties in the province had met to express their opposition to the Coercive Acts, Suffolk County had yet to convene. Representatives from the towns of the county, Boston included, would, he hoped, meet soon. But since he was likely to be in Philadelphia at the time, Adams urged Warren to take a hand in the matter to ensure the right results.

While Adams fretted about politics, some in the community worried over him. Samuel Adams never displayed much concern about his personal appearance, and it showed. Next to his elegant and stylish friends, he looked frumpy. About to venture beyond Massachusetts for the first time in his life, Adams needed to display some worldly charm. His grandson described a dinner scene at Purchase Street shortly before the departure for Philadelphia.

> A knock was heard at the door. It proved to be a well-known tailor, who politely asked that Mr. Adams should allow him to take his measure. He firmly refused to give any explanation, and finally the measure was taken, when the tailor bowed and took his leave. The family seated themselves again, and were speculating upon what this could mean, when they were attracted by another knock at the door. This time the most approved hatter in Boston introduced himself, and desired to get the size of Mr. Adams's head. He had hardly disappeared before a shoemaker came, and was followed by one or two others on similar errands, each observing a strict silence as to the persons whose orders they were obeying. A few days afterward, a large trunk was brought to the house and placed in the front entrance, directed to Mr. Samuel Adams. It contained a complete suit of clothes, two pairs of shoes of the best style, a set of silver shoe-buckles, a set of gold knee-buckles, a set of gold sleeve-buttons, an elegant cocked hat, a gold-headed cane, a red cloak, and a number of minor articles of wearing apparel. The cane and the sleeve-buttons [were] ornamented with the device of the Liberty-cap, which has led to the supposition that the gift came from the Sons of Liberty.

On Wednesday morning 10 August, there was a slight commotion in front of Thomas Cushing's house. The delegates to the Congress in Philadelphia, including the unusually well-dressed Samuel Adams, were preparing to leave. For three leisurely weeks, the Massachusetts delegates made their way south. Wherever they stopped, local Sons gathered to meet and toast the celebrated Mr. Adams.

The welcome at Carpenter's Hall in Philadelphia was not nearly so warm as the one offered by the crowds en route. Many of the delegates looked askance at the men from Massachusetts. Their radical reputation preceded them, and Adams in particular was viewed with considerable suspicion. Chief among those who harbored such doubts was Joseph Galloway of Pennsylvania, who observed of his Massachusetts colleague, "He eats little, sleeps little, thinks much, and is most decisive and indefatigable in the pursuit of his objectives."

Anticipating radical proposals from Adams, Galloway and his conservative allies struck first. Acting in his capacity as speaker, Galloway offered the Pennsylvania State House for the Congress's deliberations, a clever ploy to put the Congress under the influence of the conservative colony legislature, which had thus far been urging conciliation and loyalty to the empire. In a wink, Adams recognized the motive behind the offer and went to work lobbying for a different venue—Carpenter's Hall, the property of the Carpenter's Guild. The "mechanics and citizens in general," who were in sympathy with Adams, applauded the suggestion, and within a few days the choice was made. Congress met in Carpenter's Hall.

Having scored his first victory, Adams quickly proceeded to an even greater triumph. On the second day of the Congress, Thomas Cushing rose to move that the Congress open its sessions with a prayer. Well aware of the politics of Boston's Congregational ministers, delegates from other colonies viewed the request as a stratagem to ally God with the radical side. Arguing that there were so many religions represented in the body it would be impossible to find a common prayer, John Jay, a New York delegate, opposed the motion.

"Holding his puritan nose" Samuel Adams parried by suggesting that an Anglican preacher be called to give the prayer. He told his colleagues that he "could hear a prayer from a Gentleman of Piety and Virtue, who was at the same Time, a Friend to his Country. He was a Stranger in Philadelphia, but he had heard that Mr. Duche deserved that Character, and therefore he moved that Mr. Duche, an episcopal Clergyman, might be desired, to read Prayers before the Congress, tomorrow Morning." Joseph Reed, a Philadelphia friend of both Samuel and John Adams, remarked that Adams's move was a "Masterly stroke of Policy."

Adams's speech on behalf of Duche was one of the few times he rose in the Congress. Thomas Jefferson once remarked that Samuel Adams was "neither an eloquent nor easy speaker." Perhaps this deficiency had a great deal to do with his noticeable reticence, but his reluctance to speak also accorded with his grander plan. It was best to let his ideas come from the mouths of those not scorned for their radical reputations. Fortunately, fires were sufficiently stoked by southern delegates, Virginia and South Carolina in particular, to keep the meeting warm.

Back in Boston, the people had not been idle. Early in September, representatives from the towns of Suffolk County issued a series of 19 resolves. Drafted in the main by Joseph Warren, they were prefaced by a pledge of loyalty to the crown, but then went on to deny the legality of the Coercive Acts, called on citizens to withhold taxes, recommended a full boycott of British goods, and concluded with some veiled references to armed resistance "should our enemies [make] any sudden manoeuvers."

The resolves were laid before the Philadelphia Congress on 14 September and, according to Adams, were "read by the several members of this Body with high Applause." Despite the efforts of Galloway and others to bridle emotions, Congress was clearly deeply sympathetic with Massachusetts. John Adams remarked, "The spirit, the firmness, the prudence of our province are vastly applauded, and we are universally acknowledged, the saviours and defenders of American liberty." By a unanimous vote, Congress resolved that it most thoroughly approved "the wisdom and fortitude" of the people of Massachusetts and urged them to a "perseverance in the same firm and temperate conduct as expressed in the resolutions." Before he retired that night, John Adams wrote in his diary, "This was one of the happiest days in my life. In Congress we had generous, noble sentiments, and manly eloquence. This day convinced me that America will support Massachusetts or perish with her."

For Samuel Adams the motion for solidarity with Massachusetts was the high point of the First Continental Congress. The body continued in session for five more weeks. It passed a restrained "Declaration of Rights" and agreed to the "Association," which called for nonimportation, nonexportation, and a cessation of the slave trade. The Congress also politely petitioned the king for a redress of grievances, and in one of its final actions, agreed that unless their concerns were addressed by 10 May 1775, they would meet again in Philadelphia. Most thought that such a meeting would be unnecessary. Even if Parliament was obdurate, the king's wisdom would prevail. Little did they know that barely a month before, His Majesty had signaled his inflexibility when he wrote Lord North, "The dye is now cast. The Colonies must either submit or triumph. I do not wish to come to severer measures, but we must not retreat: by coolness and an unremitted pursuit of the measures that have been adopted I trust they will come to submit."

Adams returned to Boston on 9 November. He was welcomed as a hero. Two months earlier, he had left his town as a loved, but local leader; he returned as a national figure, precisely what Gage had feared. Samuel Adams was more dangerous than ever.

During Adams's absence, Gage had summoned the General Court to convene at Salem on 5 October. As the date drew near, the governor canceled the meeting, anticipating the ill consequences likely to result from such a gathering. The representatives ignored the dismissal, designated themselves a new body, called the Provincial Congress, elected John Hancock president, and moved their meeting place to Concord. At adjournment, they elected an executive body, the Committee of Safety, with Hancock as its president. The committee was empowered to collect military stores and mobilize the militia.

Once back in Boston, Adams resumed his responsibilities as town moderator. He had also been elected to the Provincial Congress, due to convene early in 1775 at Cambridge. In addition, as chair of the committee that parceled out donations sent from other colonies to the beleaguered Boston, he garnered considerable local influence. On top of all this, he maintained his lively correspondence with old friends in other colonies as well as some new acquaintances made in Philadelphia.

That Adams moved so easily about and conducted his business in Boston was a measure of General Gage's irresolution. Through the winter of 1774 and 1775, Gage vacillated and whined. On at least two occasions, he sent a small military force out into the countryside in a vain show of force. It accomplished nothing except to anger the locals. In the meantime, through spies, the general knew full well that the Provincial Congress, at the incessant urging of Adams and Hancock, had been gathering arms. In February the congress did gather in Cambridge. It ordered militia commanders to designate a small number of their men, usually the youngest and best armed, to stand ready to march at a "minute's warning." Even so, Gage did nothing.

As was the town's custom, people crowded into the Old South on 5 March to hear the annual Massacre Day oration. Adams's closest friend, Joseph Warren, was to deliver the speech. The meetinghouse was so crowded that Warren could not make his way through the door and he entered through a window behind the pulpit. Clad in a Roman toga, Warren made his way to the pulpit with Adams seated behind him. Seated in the pews were a large number of British officers. Adams suspected that they had been sent to disrupt the meeting.

Warren took full advantage of the high drama. Draped in his flowing toga, he waved a white handkerchief in his right hand. The speech was the typical sanguinary remembrance seasoned with a plea for rights. Most in the audience applauded, but a noticeable number of groans rose up from the redcoated guests. Despite Adams's fears, however, the officers did nothing to disrupt the speech.

On 22 March the Provincial Congress assembled in Concord. Encouraged by the general impotence of the British beyond Boston Neck as well as by support from the countryside, the Congress took on a decidedly military cast. Fifty-three articles comprising the rules and regulations of the Massachusetts army were drafted, after which it was resolved "that the present dangerous and alarming situation of our public affairs renders it necessary for this colony to make preparations for their security and defense by raising and establishing an army." Amid all this activity Adams chaired a committee assigned to enlist the aid of the Mohawks, their patriot "brothers" by informing their chief about "what our fathers in Great Britain have done and threaten to do with us."

Even before suffering this defiance from the Provincial Congress, ministers in London had decided to press Gage to act. On 27 January 1775 Lord Dartmouth dispatched orders to the governor instructing him to take measures to restore the king's authority. Gage received these orders on 14 April and immediately began his preparations.

Thanks to a web of spies on both sides of the cause, General Gage had a good sense of the situation in Concord. During the sessions of the Provincial Congress, Adams and Hancock had been houseguests of Hancock's cousin Jonas Clarke, minister of the church in Lexington. Gage was fully aware of this. He was also informed that the Provincial Congress had a store of munitions in Concord. By early April Gage had determined that he would launch a quick strike at Lexington and Concord with the intention of seizing Hancock and Adams as well as the military supplies.

Gage assigned command of the expedition to Lt. Col. Francis Smith with Maj. John Pitcairn as his second. Smith gathered companies of light infantry and grenadiers and ordered them to prepare for a march. Late in the evening of 18 April the soldiers, about seven hundred in number, were ordered to fall in on the western edge of Boston Common. The men were ordered into small boats that ferried them across the Charles River to Lechmere's Point in Cambridge. By midnight nearly all the soldiers were in ranks on the Cambridge shore and ready to march the 15 miles to Lexington.

The movement of so large a body of troops was neither unexpected nor very secret. Paul Revere, "the Patriot messenger," was awakened in his North End home and told to ride to Lexington and Concord in order to warn the countryside that the regulars were on the march. As he rowed across the Charles young Robert Newman carried his two lanterns to the belfry of the North Church. Two lanterns signaled that the British were leaving Boston "by sea," that is, across the river, rather than "by land," which would have meant marching via the Neck.

Early on the morning of the nineteenth, Revere rode up to the home of Jonas Clarke, alerting everyone that the "Regulars are Out." Within a short time he was joined by William Dawes, another patriot messenger. The two men rode on toward Concord. A few miles from the town they encountered Samuel Prescott who was returning from Lexington where he had been visiting his betrothed Lydia Mulliken. Together, the three men continued on until they encountered a British patrol. Prescott escaped by riding across country. Dawes quickly returned to Lexington. Revere was captured, held for a brief time, and then let go. He returned to Lexington where Hancock and Adams were preparing to flee.

Acting on Revere's alarm, Capt. John Parker, commander of the Lexington militia company, gathered his men on Lexington Green. They waited, but when no soldiers appeared Parker ordered his men to stand down and remain ready for the alarm. Just before dawn the drum sounded and Parker's men gathered on the green.

Precisely what happened on Lexington Green has always been a matter of some dispute. There is an apocryphal story, derived from Adams's reputation as an arch conspirator. According to this legend, as the British marched toward Captain Parker's men, Adams hid behind a nearby stone wall. As the British drew near Adams fired his pistol, causing the soldiers to believe they were being fired upon by the colonials. They returned fire and charged with bayonets. The legend tells more about the popular view of Samuel Adams than about the events on Lexington Green. No one will ever know who fired the first shot at Lexington Green.

In any event, after the skirmish on Lexington Green result-
ing in the deaths of eight Americans, the British regrouped and
marched on to Concord. In Concord Colonel Smith dispatched
soldiers to guard the North Bridge over the Concord River. At
the bridge the second encounter of the day took place as a
large body of American militia came toward the British soldiers at the bridge. This time the British were routed. Later in
the day the British began their march back to Boston following
the same route that had brought them out of the town. About a
mile east of the center of Concord, at a place called Meriam's
Corner, the British and some American militia exchanged fire
again. For the remainder of the day it was a running fight for
the British all the way back to Boston. Total British casualties
were 73 killed, 174 wounded, 26 missing. The Americans suffered 93 casualties.

Adams and Hancock were gone before shots were fired on
the green. They rode toward the town of Woburn just to the
north. From there they traveled west to Billerica, where they
spent two nights riding on to Worcester, in the central part of
Massachusetts. Within a few days, they were joined by John
Adams and Thomas Cushing. With great fanfare, the quartet
set off for Philadelphia to keep their appointment with the Second Continental Congress.

On 10 May the party reached the outskirts of Philadelphia.
For days people had been waiting to get first hand information
about the events in Lexington and Concord. It was eleven
o'clock in the morning, but despite the hour, hundreds of people formed a procession to honor the men from Massachusetts.

Among those in the crowd was the Tory refugee Judge
Samuel Curwen of Salem, Massachusetts. He observed disap-
provingly that when the gentlemen crossed into the city, "all
the bells were set to ringing and chiming, and every mark of
respect that could be was expressed." Curwen noticed also,
however, that the "distinction" lavished on the Massachusetts
delegates did not sit well with others whose arrival in the city
went virtually unnoticed. Adams sensed the jealousy and

knew that, just as in the first Congress, he must be cautious lest he needlessly offend potential allies.

The news from Massachusetts transfixed Congress and the city. The situation was in a stalemate. The British held Boston but were surrounded by an estimated twenty thousand militia from all the New England states as well as New York. Each day seemed to bring more news. In the midst of such a charged environment, the delegates set about choosing a president. After some maneuvering John Hancock was elected.

Congress then moved to adopt the army surrounding Boston, but who should command it? Thus far the fulcrum of activity had been in the North. To balance the effort and draw the South more deeply into the struggle, John Adams was convinced a southerner should take command. He rose and after a few laborious words of praise, he offered the name of George Washington. Samuel had carefully prepared for this moment. He jumped to his feet to second the nomination. No other names were presented. A unanimous vote elected Washington commander in chief.

Although it is true that Washington's military experience was limited to commanding in the Virginia militia, he was, nonetheless, well regarded by his fellow delegates. Indeed, the fact that he had served for many years in the Virginia Burgesses, as well as in the First and Second Continental Congresses, made him a person with whom other delegates felt comfortable. Congress's trust in Washington was well placed.

Everyone in the chamber celebrated Washington's election, but at least one person was disappointed. Although he clearly understood the politics of the decision, John Hancock felt slighted that his name had not at least been offered in nomination. It was particularly galling to him that the brace of Adamses rushed to support the Virginian and completely disregarded him.

Samuel Adams was jubilant. The cause of Massachusetts was now the cause of the continent. His joy was short lived. On 17 June the British assaulted the American position at

Bunker Hill overlooking Boston. Among those who had taken their place inside the hilltop redoubt was Joseph Warren. After two futile assaults with heavy losses, the British infantry finally swept through the American line. Warren was among those who fell. Samuel Adams had lost his closest friend.

Warren's death doubled Adams's resolve to continue the struggle. To many the aims of the struggle were not clear. Independence had not yet been mentioned. To have done so would have frightened off nearly everyone in the Congress. In public, Adams stressed the goal of unity, for together the colonies could force king and Parliament to negotiate terms. For the moment, at least, these terms included remaining within the empire.

Adams was patient. In describing his work in Philadelphia he told his wife that "Matters go on, though slower than One could wish, yet agreeable to my mind." By the end of July, however, Adams and the other delegates were exhausted. On 1 August Congress voted a one-month recess.

Adams took the opportunity to return home. Much had happened in his absence, and he was eager to see directly what he had thus far only read about. In company with Hancock and John Adams, he hurried north, arriving in Cambridge on 11 August.

First on Adams's agenda was his family. He hadn't seen Betsy or young Samuel since leaving Worcester in April. As usual his wife had managed well. After leaving Worcester she had settled the family in Cambridge, where they were now living.

The father prided himself on his personal rectitude, but in previous years his son had strayed from that path. Young Samuel entered Harvard with the class of 1770 and soon ran amuck. As a freshman in March 1767, he was admonished by the faculty for his "Misdemeanor in the Affair of the lewd Woman" and "for going out of Town without Leave viz to Boston where he abode a Night without going home to his Fathers house." The following year, he fell into trouble again. He stole four shillings worth of wood "which lay in the College

Yard" and "had for a considerable time before made a practice of stealing Wood and other Things from the Chambers in the College."

Samuel's success in stealing wood emboldened him to snatch a few local ducks. He dressed the ducks and then presided over a Sabbath evening feast in his chamber. The college authorities were not amused. Adams was hauled before the president and degraded six places in his class.

Despite his rocky undergraduate career, the younger Adams righted himself after graduation. At his father's urging, he studied medicine with Joseph Warren. On 19 April he was still in Boston when he was arrested by the British. Within a couple of months, however, he managed to escape. Grateful that his son was safe, Adams sought a place for him in the unfolding struggle. Thanks to the influence of his father's friends in the Provincial Congress, Dr. Adams received a surgeon's commission.

On the public front Adams was also pleased with what he found. Despite the defeat at Bunker Hill, American military fortunes were improving. Washington had taken command of the army on 3 July and morale was high. Political strength was also obvious. Taking a cue from the Continental Congress, which had advised the colonies to form governments, the people of Massachusetts reverted to a modified form of the 1691 charter with an elected Provincial Congress but no governor or lieutenant governor. The new government elected Samuel Adams secretary, a post with a modest income and light duties.

Having satisfied himself that his family was safe and the political winds were favorable in Massachusetts, Adams readied himself to return to Philadelphia. Again his friends were concerned about his image. Since he rarely left Boston, Samuel Adams was a committed pedestrian. When he rode at all, he did so in a carriage. Eighteenth-century leaders were expected to sit on horseback. Early in September, Samuel Adams took his first lessons in riding on the road to Congress. For this sedentary, overweight, middle-aged gentleman, the experience was not altogether enjoyable. He survived the torture "by the help of flannel," a generous amount of which rested between him and the saddle.

Back in Philadelphia, Adams set to work. Other delegates eager for the latest news from the North hurried over to visit with the men from Massachusetts. It was not only in the North, though, that British authority was evaporating as American opposition stiffened, even among those reluctant to move toward independence. Whether all its members approved or not, Congress had become a governing body. It had an army and a post office, negotiated treaties with Indians, borrowed money, and in general performed acts associated with a sovereign assembly.

Having launched a war, Adams's friends in Massachusetts were anxious to charge forward. Joseph Hawley of Northampton, among others, wrote to Adams of his dissatisfaction: "what is our congress about, are they dozing or amusing themselves." Impatience was clearly demonstrated when the Massachusetts's Provincial Congress replaced Thomas Cushing, who had expressed doubts about independence, with Elbridge Gerry, whose commitment to independence was unquestioned.

Adams was frustrated. "Every day's delay trys my patience," he complained. Nonetheless, he continued to prowl about carefully. Maintaining consensus, unity, and harmony was uppermost in his mind. He would do or say nothing that might send delegates scurrying in opposition.

Congress's slow pace provided Adams ample time to observe, reflect, and write. Always viewing the world through his Puritan prism, he found a good deal of the world about him objectionable. He despised, for example, the high social life enjoyed by some of the delegates, John Hancock in particular. The president made it plain that he preferred the company of wealthy Pennsylvania and New York merchants to his poorer, but stalwart New England colleagues. Despite their wealth or, perhaps, because of it, Hancock's elegant new friends were in Adams's opinion "timid . . . men, who perpetually hindered the Progress of those who would fain run in the Path of Virtue and Glory." Wealth led them to vice and their politics led them to moderation. These were the Hutchinsons and Olivers of the world in slightly altered political robes.

In the interest of unity Adams held his tongue in public, but those close to him knew his fundamental beliefs were unalterable. Liberty was a delicate flower whose very existence was constantly jeopardized by those exercising political power, and the further removed that power was from the people, the more dangerous it became. The best, indeed the only adequate, restraint was in the people as they sat in town meeting or the General Court. Each day as Adams looked about the congressional chamber, he saw men in whom he had little faith and to whom he was unwilling to grant much power. How were the colonists to win a war, remain united, and preserve liberty? The complexity of the task loomed in Adams's head.

On 17 March 1776 the British evacuated Boston. The town had little military value and the cost of holding it against an aroused countryside was too high. Convinced by now that they had a serious rebellion on their hands, the ministry laid plans for a major summer campaign against New York. Given its strategic location, that port was a vital element in the British plan to regain control of the colonies. Aware of the target, Washington ordered his army to break camp and begin the march south to defend the city.

Arms were to decide the issue; no goal short of independence seemed worth the attempt. It was, however, a momentous object, and some still questioned its wisdom and feasibility. Adams knew that the decision must be unanimous. He was willing to endure "the hardness of Mens hearts" while they struggled with the matter. He knew it would require "Time and patience to remove old prejudices, to instruct the unenlightened, convince the doubting and fortify the timid."

On 6 June 1776 Adams wrote of his impatience to James Warren: "tomorrow a Motion will be made, and a Question I hope decided, the most important that was ever agitated in America. Things will go on in the right Channel and our Country will be saved."

All went according to Adams's plan. The next day Richard Henry Lee of Virginia moved, "That these United Colonies are, and of right ought to be, free and independent States, that they are absolved from all allegiance to the British Crown, and that all political connection between them and the State of Great Britain is, and ought to be, totally dissolved." John Adams seconded the motion. A conservative faction managed to delay a vote, but the "Torrent of independence " was ultimately unstoppable.

On 11 June Congress appointed a committee to bring in a declaration that would speak to Lee's resolution. Its members were Thomas Jefferson, John Adams, Benjamin Franklin, Roger Sherman, and Robert R. Livingston. The debate continued until 2 July when the Congress voted unanimously in favor of Lee's resolution. Two days later the delegates approved the Declaration, written for the most part by Jefferson, that announced and explained their decision to a "candid world." John Adams reported the events to his wife Abigail. "You will think me transported with enthusiasm, but I am not. I am well aware of the toil and bloodshed and treasure that it will cost us to maintain this Declaration and support and defend these States. Yet through all the gloom I can see the rays of ravishing light and glory. I can see that the end is more than worth all the means; and that posterity will triumph in that day's transactions."

Cousin Samuel offered a hearty amen.

CHAPTER 11

Independence

❖
❖

On Monday morning, 12 August 1776, Adams once again took leave of Philadelphia and headed home. He had been away from his family for nearly a year and he longed to see them.

Homesickness was not the only lure pulling Adams northward. From his correspondents he had learned that certain men in the Provincial Congress and elsewhere in Massachusetts had been highly critical of him. Hancock's friends, he supposed, were spreading rumors about him. He was bent on squelching them.

The road home passed through New York. Adams arrived in the city on the fourteenth and paid a visit to Washington's headquarters. He reported that he "found the General and his family in health and spirits; every officer and soldier . . . determined."

Adams's assessment of Washington's preparedness was far off the mark. Adams was never a very good judge of military affairs. The American position at New York was precarious, and Washington's strategy for defending the city was fundamentally flawed. Within a few weeks the Continental army would be fleeing the city, barely escaping the clutches of the British army.

Continuing on his way Adams reached Dedham where his family had moved on the twenty-ninth. His visit to Boston, the first since the British had evacuated the town, was an emotional experience. The redcoats had desecrated his cherished Old South by ripping out the pews, covering the floor with dirt, and making it into a riding academy. His own house had suffered as well. Furniture was either missing or destroyed, and the interior was in shambles. Not surprisingly, houses owned by Tories had escaped damage. Most of these had been confiscated when the British had left Boston, and one, the home of Robert Hallowell, was offered to Adams. He accepted and moved in with his wife and daughter.

In Watertown, Adams met members of the Provincial Congress. He also for a brief time took up his duties as secretary of the province, signing military and privateering commissions as well as a myriad of other documents.

At the moment Adams was generally satisfied. Despite the unhappy news that Washington's army was retreating from New York, local spirits were high. The Provincial Congress had ordered militia to march to Washington's aid, and according to Adams, 5000 men had been raised with "great alacrity." Blinded by unfounded optimism, Adams went so far as to suggest to his friend Gerry, who had remained behind in Philadelphia, that "our army is upon more advantageous ground than when they were in the city of New York."

A few days later Adams returned to Philadelphia where he settled back into the congressional routine. His mood had soured. He worried about his wife, who had not yet written. Her health had been poor when he left, and his fears mounted. As for the army, the only decisive action it seemed capable of accomplishing was flight across New Jersey like hares before the British hounds. Always the Bostonian, Adams considered the people of New Jersey and Pennsylvania beneath contempt. To James Warren he wrote extolling the virtues of the citizens of Massachusetts, who had thrown the enemy out. Likewise, the brave folks in Virginia and the Carolinas had risen against tyranny. "But what will be said of Pennsylvania and the Jerseys? Have they not disgraced themselves by standing idle spectators while the enemy overran a great part of their country? ... The enemy's army were, by the last account, within sixty miles of this city. If they were as near Boston, would not our countrymen cut them all to pieces or take them prisoners?"

Adams's disillusionment did not spare the commander in chief. Adams had the odd notion that somehow the American army ought to march forward into a grand, climactic battle. Washington wisely understood the folly of bold action. In the face of so powerful an enemy, he was fortunate to have held the army together, let alone lead it in a futile assault against a vastly superior enemy. Washington had rightly fallen back on Fabian tactics until he could recruit and train an army capable of challenging the king's forces.[1]

With only Washington's crumbling army standing between them and the advancing enemy, Congress grew nervous. Some anxious members suggested fleeing Philadelphia for a safer venue. Adams scoffed at the idea, but on 12 December Congress voted to adjourn to Baltimore.

Baltimore was an unpleasant experience. Not all of the delegates removed there, so fewer members shared an increasing burden of daily tasks. Adams served on the Board of War, Medical Committee, Committee on the Northern War, Foreign Alliances, and the Committee for Procuring Cannon. Adding to his woes was the city itself. Adams's fellow New Englander, William Ellery of Rhode Island, compared living in Baltimore to being on the moon, and the eminent Dr. Benjamin Rush complained it was akin to being shut up in a convent. Expense, too, was a problem. It cost twice as much to live in Baltimore as in Philadelphia, although the City of Brotherly Love

---

[1]Quintus Fabius Maximus Verrucosus was a Roman general who fought the Carthagian general Hannibal. Fabius's forces were inferior to Hannibal's so instead of a direct attack he used his army to harass and delay. The Romans gave him the title Cunctator, Latin for delayer.

was far from inexpensive. It was an outrage to place such a high price on what Ellery called "the dirtiest Place ... [they] ... ever saw."

Barely two weeks after moving to Baltimore, delegates received good news from Trenton and Princeton. Washington's victories muted criticism of the commander in chief and relieved pressure on Philadelphia. On 27 February the delegates voted to return. No one was unhappy, least of all Adams.

Despite the victories in New Jersey, when Congress reassembled at Philadelphia in mid-March, prospects for an American victory still looked bleak. The American army was small, ill trained, and in almost all ways inferior to the British. Howe's army was poised in New York, and the general's intentions for the spring campaign remained a mystery, although everyone assumed that Philadelphia topped his list. To the north the threat was equally grave, as Gen. John Burgoyne pointed his juggernaut south for the march on Albany.

Moving had disrupted Adams's fragile correspondence with his wife. Again his concerns for her health pressed upon him. He was, however, pleased about tidings from his son, stationed at Fishkill Hospital, on the upper Hudson, as an army surgeon.

In the spring as the opposing armies stirred, Howe roused himself and laid plans to move on Philadelphia while General Burgoyne made final preparations to come south from Canada. In Congress Adams and his fellow congressmen struggled to find the means to fight a war. Secret aid from France was coming in small increments. But as the onset of hostilities drew nearer, the Americans were woefully short on supplies and men.

July 1777 was a critical month. On the fifth the Americans abandoned Fort Ticonderoga opening the way for a British advance. On the twenty-seventh General Howe, after a long delay, sailed out of New York harbor with 15,000 troops and 200 ships. Everyone assumed he was bound for Philadelphia, but whether by the Chesapeake or Delaware Bays remained a mystery.

For his part, Adams was losing faith in American commanders. Although he had been willing to grant Washington additional powers as commander in chief, questions about his ability to lead were mounting. Aside from the relatively minor victories at Trenton and Princeton, Washington thus far had spent most of his efforts on retreating. As for the northern theater, Adams was even more dismayed. The news from Ticonderoga confirmed his already low opinion of the commander of that area, Gen. Philip Schuyler. Indeed, only days before Fort Ticonderoga fell, Schuyler's rival for the northern command, Gen. Horatio Gates, had been at Congress complaining bitterly about his boss. Gates's arguments made sense to Adams then; they made even more now. Thanks to strong support from the New England delegations, which had a good deal to fear from the British advance, Schuyler was dismissed and Gates took command of the northern army.

Adams had been one of Gates's chief advocates. He supported him in part because of his disdain for Schuyler, but he may also have looked upon Gates as an alternative to Washington. Four years older than Washington and a more experienced officer, Gates was born in England, the son of the Duke of Leeds's housekeeper. He entered the British army at an early age and enjoyed a distinguished career. He retired to Virginia in 1772 where he bought land. Shortly after Washington's appointment as commander in chief, Congress commissioned Gates a brigadier general and since May 1776 he had served with the northern army.

Performance was only one element in Adams's growing skepticism of Washington. Samuel Adams rarely trusted anyone who had power, particularly those who enjoyed exercising it in a grand manner. Style and elegance ran counter to his puritanical notions of simplicity and virtue. Astride a white horse, finely uniformed, surrounded by his staff equally well dressed, Washington was fast becoming the antithesis of Adams's image of the proper revolutionary leader.

John Hancock, of course, had long ago achieved that status. Since he had returned to Philadelphia, Hancock's lifestyle had grown ever more elegant. During the summer months, Hancock and several of his friends gathered at least once a week for an evening of lavish drinking and eating. Such extravagance never sat well with Adams, but in the midst of public want, it seemed all the more outrageous. Hancock, however, brushed off any criticism. "I have Expended my own money," he declared, and "in that case had a Right to drink wine if I pleased."

Meanwhile the British marched on. On 11 September Howe defeated Washington at Brandywine. Fearing again that the city might fall, Congress fled once more, this time to York, Pennsylvania, a place so remote and provincial that it made some members yearn for Baltimore. Less than a week later, Washington moved his army to launch an attack against the British at Germantown. Again the Americans were defeated, although Washington did manage to maintain his army intact and withdraw in good order. No optimistic view could deny, however, that, Philadelphia was now in enemy hands.

Amid such disheartening events came jubilant news from General Gates. In a series of battles around Saratoga, New York, he had defeated Burgoyne and accepted the surrender of his entire army. Gates's star was rising rapidly above the horizon.

In a somber mood several members of Congress took their leave of York and headed for home. Among those departing was the president. Never one to humble himself, Hancock insisted on making a farewell speech. In the short history of Congress, no member had ever demanded such recognition. Hoping that granting him an audience would end this round of Hancockian posturing, the president's critics suffered silently through the address. To their disgust, however, at the end of the speech, a delegate moved that "the thanks of Congress be presented to John Hancock." Adams was outraged. Claiming it was "improper to thank any president for the discharge of the duties of that office," he registered a strong objection. Adams's logic was sound. Only six states could be mustered in support of the motion. Leading the opposition was Massachusetts, where every delegate, Hancock excepted, stood with Adams. Hancock would not forget this slight from his "friends."

Less than two weeks after Hancock's unhappy departure, Samuel and John Adams set out on the road to Boston. They made a wide swing north until they ferried over the Hudson at Fishkill. The detour had a special attraction, for Dr. Samuel Adams was there along with William Eustis, another Boston physician trained under Joseph Warren. On 4 December, after more than three weeks on the road, Adams arrived home.

Like the prophet Jeremiah who preached doom to ancient Israel, Adams lamented the state of his community. He was distressed at the fawning over Gen. John Burgoyne and his officers who had been marched to Boston, where they served as gaudy ornaments available to decorate any social event. Adams was aghast at such frivolity and worried incessantly about the "Contagion of Vice" carried by Burgoyne and his officers. When the issue was moral declension, however, Adams always feared internal corrosion over external attack. The Burgoyne infection would be purged as soon as the general and his troops made their way home. Indigenous vices required a more powerful physic.

Once independence had been declared it fell to the states to fashion new, sovereign governments. There was never any doubt, at least in Massachusetts, that such a new government must have a written constitution. Since 1629 the colony had been governed under a written document. The same was true for most of the other colonies as well. Unlike their British cousins, who had no single written "constitution," the people of America were accustomed and expected their governments to have a document in which rights, privileges, and powers were explicitly set out. On 4 April 1777 the Massachusetts House of Representatives resolved "to empower the General Court to frame a Constitution," which, when completed, would be submitted to the towns for approval. Adams feared the result.

The form of government was always less important to Samuel Adams than the people within it. Any government, no matter how well intentioned or cleverly crafted, could be corrupted by evil people. And evil was certainly not in short supply in Boston. Speculation, inflation, and greed were abetted by public apathy. Given what he had seen in Congress Adams cast a jaundiced eye toward his old nemesis, Hancock, who was likely to be chosen chief magistrate. Firmly believing that the person chosen "will in a great Measure form the Morals and Manners of the People," Adams was decidedly displeased. Yet what could he do? Along with James Warren and a few other "old revolutionaries," Adams argued for a return to communal virtue and the Puritan ethic. A few listened but most swooned before the largesse of Hancock who supplied firewood for the almshouse and opened his ample purse to the poor. Adams sputtered.

Adams had political problems of his own as well. Rumors, spread mostly by supporters of Hancock, linked him to a conspiracy against Washington. Whispered allegations set among those who questioned the commander in chief's competence. Washington had lost New York and Philadelphia; been defeated at Brandywine and Germantown, and by late 1777 was withdrawing into winter quarters with a weakened and demoralized army. In contrast, Gen. Horatio Gates, a favorite of Adams and the New Englanders, had turned in a brilliant victory at Saratoga. Small wonder that when a certain letter, written by Maj. Gen. Thomas Conway, a friend and supporter of Gates, came to light some men questioned Washington's leadership. The letter disparaged Washington and exalted Gates. It caused a considerable stir in Congress, but in the end, congressional support for Washington never wavered.

Because Adams had already expressed his concerns over Washington's failures and that several of his close associates had been rumored to be part of a conspiracy, Hancock found it very easy to implicate Adams. The charges struck a nerve. Beginning with his arrival home in December 1777, when the allegations first appeared, and continuing throughout the rest of his life, these stories bedeviled Samuel Adams.

Adams's stay at home was pleasant enough. After recovering from an illness that laid him low in January, he attended to his business as secretary. He remained aloof from local politics. In February, he joined with a host of others to bid farewell to John Adams, Congress's newly appointed commissioner to France, and his 10-year-old son, John Quincy, as they embarked for Bordeaux on a mission which took on added significance when news arrived that the French were ready to strike an alliance with the United States.

Except for defending his reputation from Hancockian allegations and carping to his friends and in the press about high prices and a universal lack of public virtue, Adams did little in public during his stay at home. He supported, but did not take an active role in, the approval of the Articles of Confederation, which he had helped write in Congress. He also watched, but did not participate in the debates over the state constitution, a document that eventually went down to defeat in July.

By early May Adams was ready to return to Congress. After several days on the road, he wrote to Betsy from the town of Palmer, about 100 miles west of Boston. He already missed his home and family:

> This Afternoon I met my Son on the Road. I was sorry I could not have the Pleasure of conversing with him. I parted with him with great Regret. May Heaven bless him! Tell him I shall never think him too old to harken to the Advice of his Father. Indeed I never had Reason to complain of him on that Account. He has hitherto made me a glad Father. This implys that I esteem him a wise Son. I have been more sparing of Advice to him because I have thought he did not need it; but in these critical Times when *Principles & Manners* as well as the *Liberties of his Country* are in Danger he has need to be on his Guard.

A reconvened Congress had much to celebrate. With the French alliance secured, military fortunes took on a promising aspect. By midsummer a French fleet was off the coast, and after an unsuccessful attempt at New York the fleet rendezvoused with an American army at Newport to launch an attack on the British there. Poor coordination, British resolve, and bad weather combined to thwart the expedition.

Publicly Adams supported the alliance with France. He was realist enough to know that foreign assistance was vital to American success; nonetheless, the arrangement made him uneasy. He held a New Englander's historical antipathy toward French Catholicism. He wanted French money and guns but abhorred the potential influence on his community.

Adams's views toward America's ally became apparent in yet another congressional spat. Early in the war Congress had dispatched Benjamin Franklin, Arthur Lee, Adams's good friend and confidant, and Silas Deane to France as commissioners. It did not take long before the three men fell out, Lee on one side, Franklin and Deane on the other. In letters home, Lee accused Deane of a cozy relationship with French merchants that he exploited for his own financial gain. Lee's accusations resulted in Deane's being recalled to answer charges before Congress.

Deane's appearance at Congress raised a row that did not subside for months. His supporters, mainly pro-French and mercantile, could not see that he had done anything wrong. His opponents, including Adams, suspected Deane of cupidity and were all wary of the French. The new French minister to Congress, Conrad Gerard, understood Adams to be an adversary and used his influence to undermine him.

Adams did what he could to persuade the people that he was not anti-French. His attempts were thwarted, however, when it came to light that he had been in private conversation with a British agent, John Berkenhout, and, even worse, that he had been talking with John Temple, the former royal customs commissioner in Boston.

Samuel Adams lived in two political worlds—Philadelphia and Boston. By late 1778 his influence in both was in decline.

Adams's congressional life had become increasingly fractious. He saw around him not the patriots with whom he had begun the great adventure of revolution, but greedy, self-interested men, devoted more to power and profit than to liberty and virtue. He described them as "a Combination of political & Commercial Men, who may be aiming to get the Trade, the Wealth, the Power and the Government of America into their own Hands."

Power was most dangerous and difficult to control when it was concentrated. Lots of debate and plural participating committees diffused the threat. Having been raised with a profound respect for town meeting, Adams saw it as the proper model for government while others did not. Evidence that it was not working in Philadelphia was overwhelming. Committees, including the Marine Committee that Adams chaired, could not even summon enough members for a quorum. Endless debate over trivial issues consumed hours; important decisions were left embedded in an ever lengthening, untended agenda. The Congress, according to John Jay, was suffering from "Want of [a] System."

To Adams the implication behind Jay's criticism smacked of what he feared most—concentration of power in the wrong hands that would inevitably lead to encroachment on the rights of states. Adams warned against that evil, but in the face of mounting examples of congressional ineptitude, his stand was increasingly unpopular. The direction was clear: Congress would gradually abandon the town meeting style of government and move toward concentrating authority in the hands of elected boards and officials. Adams dissented.

In Boston, matters were not much better. Samuel Adams and John Hancock were different in many ways, but in no instance were they further apart than in their capacity for reconciliation. Hancock could be flexible and forgiving. Adams was rarely either. It was a political liability from which he suffered greatly.

Samuel Phillips Savage, a friend to both Adams and Hancock, was distressed over the breach between them. He wrote to Adams,

> as much as I value you my Country lies nearer my heart, and
> I greatly fear the differences now subsisting between you
> and your once friend Mr. H. may greatly hurt her interest.

> The enemies of America triumph in the Strife and are taking every measure to encrease the Flame. The Friends of their Country see the encreasing Contest with weeping eyes and aching hearts and wish a Reconciliation. Permit me my Friend to attempt (however inadequate to the Task) a Restoration of Friendship between two who once were dear to each other and who now perhaps from mistakes and misapprehensions seem so distant.

Adams's frigid response left no room for accord.

> You call upon me by all that is sacred to forgive him. Do you think he has injured me? If he has, should he not ask for forgiveness? No man ever found me inexorable. I do not wish him to ask me to forgive him; this would be too humiliating. If he is conscious of having done or designed me an injury, let him do so no more, and I will promise to forgive and forget him too; or would I add, to do him all the service in my power. But this is needless; it is not in my power to serve him. *He* is above it.

Adams was tired, and so the news that he had been reelected to Congress for 1779 came as a mixed blessing. He wanted to be at home but agreed to serve at least until the spring, when he hinted that he would return to Boston.

By the time spring arrived, Adams was ready to come home. In June he settled in with his family and resumed his light duties as secretary to the Provincial Congress, and member of the Board of War, offices that made him uncomfortable. The provincial government had never been intended as a permanent body. Formed first as an ad hoc structure in the confused days of 1774 and 1775 it was de facto government, although the people of Massachusetts had never in any formal sense approved of it; therefore it lacked "legitimacy." With ties to king and parliament irrevocably severed, the people of Massachusetts decided to look to themselves for a new form of governance.

In the spring of 1778, the General Court had written and sent to the people a proposed state constitution. Citing a number of deficiencies, not the least a lack of a bill of rights, the towns rejected it. The legislature opted to try again, but this time the task would be given to a special convention elected for the purpose. The people of Boston elected Adams as one of 12 delegates to represent them at the convention. Although the actual drafting of the constitution fell to a small number of men—John and Samuel Adams and James Bowdoin being among the most active—the document itself reflected the collective colonial and revolutionary experience of the people of Massachusetts. Care was given to listen to and incorporate the ideas of delegates from all parts of the state.

Much of the writing bears the imprint of John Adams; still it was evident that the elder Adams had a strong influence. The "Preamble" set a mood, Puritan in tone, that suffused the document.

> The body politic is formed by a voluntary association of individuals; it is a social compact, by which the whole people covenants with each citizen, and each citizen with the whole people, that all shall be governed by certain laws for the common good. It is the duty of the people, therefore, in framing a constitution of government, to provide for an equitable mode of making laws, as well as for an impartial interpretation, and a faithful execution of them; that every man may, at all times, find his security in them.

Recognizing that the previous effort at shaping a constitution for the state had collapsed in part because of the lack of a bill of rights, this effort began with just such a declaration. Thirty articles listed the rights of the people. Article III, written by Samuel Adams, asserted that "as the happiness of people, and the good order and preservation of civil government, essential depend upon piety, religion, and morality." To guarantee their existence in the new commonwealth this article went on to require public support for churches and to provide "for the support and maintenance of public Protestant teachers of piety, religion and morality." Among other things the bill also guaranteed freedom of speech, freedom of the press, the right to keep and bear arms, and the right of assembly and petition.

Articles IV and V affirmed Adams's most deep-seated beliefs about the nature of government.

> Article IV. The people of this commonwealth have the sole and exclusive right of governing themselves, as a free, sovereign, and independent state; and do, and forever hereafter shall, exercise and enjoy every power, jurisdiction, and right, which is not, or may not hereafter, be by them expressly delegated to the United States of America in Congress assembled.

> Article V. All power residing originally in the people, and being derived from them, the several magistrates and officers of government, vested with authority, whether legislative, executive, or judicial, are their substitutes and agents, and are at all times accountable to them.

This was the commonwealth's solemn compact to maintain a community rooted in piety, religion, and morality. Samuel Adams was less interested in the form of the government. He left that to his lawyerly cousin John. He was more interested that the form be one in which public virtue ruled.

John Adams did provide the detail in a form pleasing to Samuel. The Massachusetts constitution of 1780 provided for a two-house legislature, an executive, and a judiciary. It also provided for property qualifications exceeding those in effect under the king, thus excluding considerable numbers from the electorate. By every measure, this constitution aimed to stem the democratic impulses let loose by the Revolution, and given the public dissipation he had witnessed, Samuel Adams accepted such restrictions. The people, he had by now concluded, could not always be trusted to do the right thing and needed to be monitored by those wiser and more virtuous. Adams well understood that wisdom and virtue were not inherited traits. A good government would strive to instruct its people in their acquisition. He claimed,

> Wise and judicious Modes of Education, patronized, and supported by communities, will draw together the Sons of the rich, and the poor, among whom it makes no distinction; it

will cultivate the natural Genius, elevate the Soul, excite laudable Emulation to excel in Knowledge, Piety, and Benevolence, and finally it will reward its Patrons, and Benefactors by shedding its benign Influence on the Public Mind.

In Adams's view this new covenant, the constitution of 1780, did all he could wish. It established a mixed form of government wherein power was diffused and virtue supported. It provided for a commonwealth founded on the optimistic notion that virtue and piety could be learned, tempered by the sober recognition that government must also be able "to check the human Passions, and control them from rushing into exhorbitances."

For the most part, the people of Massachusetts agreed with Samuel Adams. On 2 March the constitution was sent out "to be laid before the inhabitants." After weeks of confused voting, the convention reconvened, reviewed the returns, and proclaimed that the constitution is "passed in the affirmative by a very great majority."

Having completed his work at home, Adams prepared to return to Congress. It had never been easy to say good-bye, but this time it was even more difficult. Shortly before he left, Thomas Wells, his wife's younger brother, sought a few moments of his time. He asked leave to marry Hannah, Adams's daughter by Elizabeth Checkley. Despite the age difference Samuel was pleased. What better family could his daughter find? He offered his blessing. The marriage was set for a year hence.

By the summer of 1780 Congress's eyes were focused on the South. Charleston had fallen to the British in May, and Gen. Charles Cornwallis had moved inland. Adams's old friend Horatio Gates had been dispatched to take command. In a series of battles, Cornwallis routed Gates and sent him fleeing in retreat. Dismayed at Gates's failure, Congress ordered Gen. Nathanael Greene to take command. Greene proved an able leader and by late 1780 Cornwallis's forces were showing signs of fatigue and despair.

Although he was disappointed by Gates, Adams was pleased that Greene had resurrected the southern campaign.

With Great Britain now facing enemies in Europe, Adams hoped its efforts in America might weaken. He joined with other members of Congress in placing great store in the French fleet. If it could get to America, important goals might be accomplished. In the meantime Greene must be encouraged to continue his attacks on Cornwallis.

Meanwhile, affairs in Massachusetts wore a different aspect. As usual Adams worried over the moral state of his commonwealth. In October the first elections were held under the new constitution. To no one's surprise, John Hancock was elected governor. To the surprise of some, however, Adams failed to be elected to any post in the new government. Adams was circumspect. Despite proddings from his wife and the ever critical James Warren, he offered no condemnation of either the governor or the people. He was, he told Betsy, content to accept the judgment of the people. He even hinted that perhaps it was time to seek the "Sweets of Retirement."

In the spring of 1781, as the weather turned fair, Adams made plans to return home. Early in May he left Philadelphia for the last time. Thereafter he concentrated his attention on affairs in the "narrower Compass" of the new commonwealth.

CHAPTER 12

The New Republic

❖
❖

While Samuel Adams had the joy of being present at the creation of the commonwealth, he soon realized that he did not control it. Hancock's overwhelming victories were proof that Adams's foes were in complete control of the new government.

In his usual dour fashion, James Warren lamented the sad state of affairs to Adams, who had returned to Philadelphia. Even in his darkest moods, Samuel Adams never sank to the depths of despondency in which Warren wallowed. In his response to Warren, Adams was philosophical. Even "an honest & virtuous People" were capable of error, he acknowledged. Certainly they had acted "with their Eyes open." Although now they would soon learn the folly of their ways and strike a path toward virtue. Adams shared St. Paul's view "that tribulation produces endurance, and endurance proven virtue, and proven virtue hope."

But Adams continued to hope. Over time the citizens of Massachusetts showed no sign that they had tired of Hancock's parade. With the exception of only two years, occasions when he chose not to run, John Hancock was reelected handily to be first magistrate of the commonwealth from 1780 to 1793.

Edged out of affairs at home and in Philadelphia by his enemies Adams felt increasingly marginalized. Impoverished, ill organized, and lacking talent, Congress was having trouble seeing beyond the Revolution. Trying to resuscitate the body, some members of Congress advocated concentrating authority in the hands of boards and executives. Adams opposed the proposal, which offended his sense of town meeting government. Despite his qualms, in February 1781 Robert Morris was made superintendent of finance. Soon he would control a good deal of what had formerly been done on the floor of Congress.

While the appointment of the ambitious Morris was no cause for celebration, Adams was pleased that after a five-year struggle, on 1 March the Articles of Confederation were finally ratified. Conceived in the heady atmosphere of 1776 and approved by Congress in 1777, the Articles created a confederation of equal states tied together by little more than goodwill. This was as Adams had wished. Four years later, when disillusioned state governments and the Congress itself were moving away from the philosophy underpinning the confederation, the Articles were law. Adams failed to see the irony.

In June Adams made the trek northward. When he arrived home, he was pleased to learn that he had been reelected to the state senate. As soon as that body met, the senators would choose Adams as their president, a position of dignity but little authority. Samuel Adams was, in the eyes of his fellow countrymen, fast becoming an icon to be venerated but not entrusted with power.

Although it was never in his character to be completely happy, the early 1780s would later spark pleasant memories. In October 1781 news of Yorktown signaled an effective end of the war and the onset of serious negotiations for peace. Adams rejoiced over the victory, and in the blush of events, he even found hope at home. He pinned his faith not on the government of the commonwealth, led by a popinjay governor, but on the people, whose good sense endured. To John Adams, who was at the Hague haggling with Dutch burghers over a loan, he wrote, "Matters go on here as you would expect from your knowledge of the People. Zealous in the great Cause, they hesitate at no Labor or Expense for its Support."

What united the "People" was the "great Cause." That cause, American independence, concluded with the Treaty of Paris, signed 3 September 1783 and ratified by Congress on 14 January 1784. The discipline of war had held the common-wealth and nation together. Adams was not certain that same unity would prevail in peace.

In the midst of this anticipation the Adams family moved into a new house once owned by Sylvanus Gardiner, a refugee Tory. An old structure, built early in the eighteenth century, it had three stories, heavily timbered and sided with yellow clapboards that seemed always to be in need of a coat of paint. On the first floor were two large parlors with a kitchen at the back opening onto a bricked courtyard. Neither the house nor the neighborhood had a hint of elegance, but here Adams, sur-rounded by "etchings of eminent Americans" as well as two full-sized portraits of himself and his wife, received guests and discussed politics.

For Massachusetts, as well as its sister states, the postwar world was a troubled place. Public and private debt from the war weighed heavily on the commonwealth and its citizens. Farmers in the western counties grumbled about high taxes and heavy mortgages. In the east merchants caviled against a hostile British trade policy that dumped cheap goods on Boston wharves but made it difficult to send American goods in the other direction. As president of the senate, Adams was well aware of the problems, and in the summer of 1782 he journeyed west to Hatfield along with Artemus Ward to meet a delegation of disgruntled farmers.

The situation called for strong action from the state gov-ernment, but Governor Hancock, relying on his charm and his political managers to keep him in office, was not motivated to respond. Although the commonwealth was approaching fi-nancial ruin, the governor never once presented a plan to re-store it to fiscal well-being. Hancock's indecision and feeble leadership were disturbing, and the people were beginning to express their dissatisfaction. From 1781 to 1784, Hancock scored fewer votes each time the freemen went to the polls.

Among Hancock's most effective critics was Adams's friend Mercy Otis Warren, James Otis's sister and James Warren's wife. Mrs. Warren rarely missed an opportunity for a caustic remark upon Hancock's character. She viewed him as a vacillating incompetent with feet of clay and a head to match. Picturing themselves as "the lovers of the early revolutionary principles ... [and] lovers of virtue," Mrs. Warren and others, including Adams, were among the most implacable of Hancock's foes.

Unfortunately, virtue and early revolutionary principles did not sell at the polls. Hancock's machine rolled on to victory, and Adams found himself, as he had often in his career, a carping outsider preaching ancient values derived from the Puritan compact to an audience deaf to his pleadings.

In February 1785 Adams and his allies got some unexpected good news. Because of ill health, John Hancock had resigned the governorship. Running in Hancock's stead was his staunch friend Thomas Cushing. His opponent was James Bowdoin, a rich, well-born, conservative merchant. He was just the sort of man Adams distrusted before the war, but his conservative views now resonated well with this "old revolutionary."

The possibility of turning out the Hancockians energized Adams. With public virtue still in decline, Adams seized upon the election as a moment to rejuvenate old values. His strategy centered on the issue of a Tea Assembly.

The winter of 1784–1785 was especially long and severe, and several prominent citizens of Boston had organized themselves into a Tea Assembly, or social club, where they could periodically gather during those dreary winter months and enjoy an evening of dancing and card playing. Adams was horrified. Dubbed by him and others the "Sans Souci" (Without Care), the club represented the moral degeneracy and decline of republican virtue he had always associated with the Hancockians. A series of attacks, most likely written by Adams, was launched in the *Massachusetts Centinel*.

The first salvo from the pen of "Observer" hit the mark: "reason bewildered, and stupefied by dissipation and extrava-

gance. Did ever effeminacy with her languid train receive a
greater welcome in society than at this day. . . . We are prosti-
tuting all our glory as a people for new modes of pleasure ru-
inous in their expenses, injurious to virtue, and totally detri-
mental to the well being of society."

. Extending well beyond the Tea Assembly, "the issue was
nothing less than the nature of American society." Samuel
Adams's revolution was in danger of failing. He had fought
for independence against a corrupt British regime so he might
lead his people back to their origins, the old Puritan covenant
based on John Winthrop's vision of a godly community. Released from bondage, however, the people showed little inclination to follow Adams back to his Zion in the wilderness.
They preferred instead the more secular and acquisitive future
symbolized by John Hancock.

Through the winter of 1785, "Observer" relentlessly assailed the vanity, extravagance, and immorality prevailing in
Boston, an excess epitomized by "Sans Souci." Adams's
friend Mercy Otis Warren joined in the fray with *A Farce,* a
short play parodying some of the more aristocratic citizens of
Boston under such names as Mr. Importance, Madame Brilliant, and Mr. Bon Ton.

The people listened. Bowdoin easily won the election of
1785, particularly in Boston where his margin was two to one
over Cushing. One of the first acts of the new governor was to issue "A Proclamation for the Encouragement of Piety, Virtue, Education and Manners, and for the Suppression of Vice." Not long
after, he presented a plan for fiscal reform, something the General
Court had never received from Hancock. In the fall the governor
called for a national meeting to consider measures to regulate
American commerce. In Bowdoin's administration Adams saw
hope. It was, he told John Adams, "what I have long wishd for."

However, virtue was not the most important issue facing
the commonwealth. Romantic notions of "republican virtue"
blinded both Adams and Bowdoin to the political realities of a
state in distress. As easterners, both men failed to hear the
pleas of debt-ridden western farmers.

With Boston ignoring their plight, men in the central and western counties took matters into their own hands. Between July 1786 and February 1787 they gathered at least eight times in county conventions and petitioned the General Court for reform. Some easterners questioned the loyalty of the presumptuous westerners, and a note of hysteria about the conventions began to creep into conversation. Those who had once led a revolution now lived in fear that they would be the target of one. It did not go unnoticed that little more than a decade before, "county conventions" had been a prelude to Lexington and Concord.

By fall, armed mobs had appeared in Worcester, Middlesex, Bristol, Hampshire, and Berkshire counties. Their immediate goal was always the same: to close down the courts in order to halt legal proceedings against debtors. These actions alarmed Bowdoin, who asked the General Court for extraordinary powers, including the right to suspend habeas corpus, so the courts might restore order. In the House, where westerners had considerable influence, his requests were tabled, whereas in the more conservative and eastern-dominated Senate, where Adams sat, they were warmly received. Indeed, during that fall, Bowdoin called on Adams frequently for advice and support, of which he got in abundance.

In early December, the violence that had hitherto been sporadic and uncoordinated became more organized. Under the leadership of Capt. Daniel Shays, a former officer of the Continental army, the insurgents tried to seize the arsenal at Springfield. They were repulsed by state militia. A few days later Gen. Benjamin Lincoln arrived with a force dispatched by Bowdoin. Lincoln pursued the Shaysites and smashed them at Petersham. Shays fled to Vermont, and his followers scattered.

Daniel Shays did to Samuel Adams what Thomas Hutchinson could never do. Even in the darkest days of the 1760s and early 1770s, moments when Adams openly despised Hutchinson and his ilk, he never lost his temper, never sank to the depths of anger and hate that now consumed him. Once the convulsions in the countryside had been calmed, most leaders in the commonwealth were content to offer leniency and forgiveness to Shays's followers. Not so for Adams. When Bowdoin inquired of his friend if he should grant pardons, Adams shot back that the governor ought "to inflict that just, condign punishment which the judicial sentence had awarded on the detestable leaders of that banditti who raised the rebellion. In monarchies the crime of treason and rebellion may admit of being pardoned or lightly punished; but the man who dares to rebel against the laws of the republic ought to suffer death." Fortunately, cooler heads prevailed. No one was executed and in the spring of 1787 Hancock was returned as governor and Adams was reelected to the Senate. Just as Hancock was once more taking the reins in Massachusetts, an even grander event got underway in Philadelphia.

To his credit, James Bowdoin had been among the first to urge a national initiative on trade. However, the issues facing the Confederation transcended commerce and reached far into more political realms. Increasingly, men both within and without Congress sought to craft a stronger national government. Representatives of Virginia, New York, New Jersey, Delaware, and Pennsylvania met at Annapolis in September 1786 to discuss subjects of mutual concern. That meeting spawned plans for another gathering to be held at Philadelphia to which all the states were invited to send representatives. The call was sent out by the Congress and advertised as an occasion to discuss and perhaps reform the Articles. The representatives convened on 25 May, elected Washington their chair, and then proceeded to write a new constitution. They finished their work in September and dispatched the document to the states for ratification by special conventions. As soon as nine states ratified, the Constitution of the United States would become a reality.

When Hancock received the Constitution he summoned a joint session of the Senate and House. Adams listened as His Excellency made a few perfunctory remarks about the excellent character of the men who had produced the document. He said nothing to reveal his own position.

While Hancock was silent, Adams expressed his reservations. He shared his doubts with his old friend Richard Henry Lee. He could not understand why the Convention had chosen "a National Government, instead of a Federal Union of Sovereign States. If the several States in the Union are to become one entire Nation, under one Legislature, the Powers of which shall extend to every Subject of Legislation, and its Laws be supreme & control the whole, the Idea of Sovereignty in these States must be lost." Herein was Adams's dilemma. He believed that even when his fellow citizens strayed, à la "Sans Souci," they would, like the prodigal son, return home. Because they shared a common tradition, their compass needle would, no matter what the temporary deviation, always swing back to a course of virtue, piety, and covenant. What Adams refused to believe was that others did not necessarily own the same compass. Citizens in the various states had different "Habits and Interests." They had a different history. Content in his provinciality, Adams had no desire to impose on them his own views; he feared that this new document would allow them to impose their views on him. In effect, he could not reconcile the size and diversity of the proposed union with the preservation of his particular and unique community.

Adams was not alone in his concerns; others also doubted the wisdom of a federal union. Many critics of the Constitution, including Adams's friend Elbridge Gerry, who had been a Massachusetts delegate to the convention and had refused to sign the Constitution, charged that republics were incapable of governing geographically large and diverse areas. Only authoritarian regimes, like ancient Rome, could sustain the power necessary to bring order to such a vast and diverse area as that represented by the proposed new nation. Wherever the interests of the nation at large conflicted with a smaller community, the interests of the nation would always ride roughshod over the states.

Massachusetts elections for the ratifying convention were held and the date for the first meeting was set for 2 January 1788. Among the delegates from Boston were Adams, Hancock, and Bowdoin. A few days before the opening session, Bowdoin invited the 11 other delegates to dinner where he planned to thump for ratification. The evening did not go according to his plan. Hancock and another delegate, John Winthrop, stayed home. The remaining ten supped well, but then Adams broke the calm by suggesting that he had strong reservations about supporting ratification, but added he was "open to conviction." Ironically, Hancock's oblique tilting against ratification and Adams's expressed reservations now provided a common ground on which the two old antagonists finally stood together.

From the moment the convention opened, it was clear that the Federalist and anti-Federalist forces were fairly evenly balanced. The Federalists could claim the greater talent and money. Their side was heavily endowed with lawyers, judges, politicians, and others of the "better sort." The resources of the anti-Federalists were more modest, but their numbers were nearly equal to the Federalists.

In the opening debates, Adams, preferring to be an "auditor" rather than an "objector," took a neutral position. He did, however, deign to attend, unlike his erstwhile friend John Hancock, who also harbored serious doubts. Even though the convention elected him president, the governor claimed illness, reclined at home on Beacon Hill, and remained silent.

The silence of Adams and Hancock was troubling. No two men were more revered in the commonwealth. Their opinions carried great weight.

If Hancock would not come down off the hill, then the Federalists would go to him. Delegations trudged up Beacon Hill. Hoping he might see the necessity for ratification they flattered and cajoled him. Hints of fame and of national office—possibly the presidency—were thrown out, possibilities that depended on ratification. He listened.

Adams too was wooed. Unmoved by promises of grandeur, he was more likely to be swayed by a common appeal. He had been told by some that a goodly number of Boston mechanics were opposed to the Constitution. These men and their fathers had formed the stiff backbone of resistance in the days of the Revolution. When pusillanimous merchants were grasping for compromise, these men had stood with Adams. He would not desert them now.

Knowing Adams's sympathies, the Federalists sought a mechanic who might influence him in their favor. Who better to argue the case before Adams than Paul Revere, the best known mechanic of the town, a man whose revolutionary credentials were impeccable? At the urging of Revere and other leading mechanics, a mass meeting was held at the Green Dragon Tavern. The overflowing crowd shouted support for a resolution endorsing the Constitution and then appointed a delegation led by Revere to carry the news to Adams. The men marched down Orange Street toward Winter Street. Adams invited Revere and a few others into his home.

"How many," asked Adams, "were gathered together when this resolution was passed?"
"More, sir, than the Green Dragon could hold."
"And where were the rest, Mr. Revere?"
"In the streets, sir."

Adams was moved by the common people's apparent support for the Constitution and by their affection for him. Nonetheless, he still hesitated. By nature he was suspicious of power, and in his judgment, as well as that of Hancock, the Constitution granted the proposed federal government too much authority with too few restrictions.

Conscious of their roles in the unfolding drama, the two revolutionaries seemed to draw closer together. Perhaps, having worked side by side to destroy one imperium, they now rallied jointly to the task of creating a new one. The emotions drawing them closer may also have been more basic. On 17 January, after a long and painful illness, Samuel Adams's only son died in his father's house. The event transpired almost one year to the day of the death of Hancock's only son, 12-year-old John George Washington Hancock. Such a fundamental loss united the fathers in their grief.

Hancock sent a note of condolence to Adams. This personal reconciliation helped open a pathway toward political rapprochement. As they talked, Hancock and Adams came to appreciate that they shared a common vision for the new nation and its constitution. They wanted a union of sovereign states. The states would protect the liberties of the people, and the nation would defend the whole. They worried that the document presented allowed too great an intrusion into matters belonging to the state. Closeted together in the younger man's Beacon Hill mansion, Adams and Hancock did again what they had done so well two decades before; they laid plans.

Both men understood that a defeat for the Constitution would be irreparable. If the states failed to choose unity, disunity would be the inevitable result. Whatever faults the plan for a new nation might contain, the threat of a divided nation was a danger of much greater magnitude. To satisfy themselves, as well as others who shared their concerns, Adams and Hancock agreed on a list of amendments designed to protect the rights of states and citizens against a powerful central government.

Adams believed it would be far more effective if the governor himself should speak to the convention, and so, after his long absence from the deliberations, Hancock made a dramatic appearance on Thursday afternoon, 31 January. Adams was present when Hancock took the chair and rose to speak. The audience fell silent. It was his hope, Hancock informed them, that the convention would ratify the document. He realized it was not perfect and that some were anxious about certain omissions. He proposed, therefore, a series of amendments "in order to remove the doubts, and quiet the apprehensions." He suggested a list of nine amendments, the sum total of which had the effect of curbing, but not crippling, the federal government. Many of these amendments, along with those proposed by other state conventions, would later be forwarded to the First Congress where they were sifted and bundled together as the Bill of Rights.

As Hancock resumed his seat, Adams rose to speak. For the first time in years, he stood with the governor and saluted his "Excellency's conciliatory proposition." Save the occasion when they had risked their lives to vote independence, this may well have been their finest hour.

Despite approval of the Constitution by Adams and Hancock, a sizable number of people feared the prospect of a federal government. When the final vote was taken, ratification carried by only a narrow margin of 187 to 168.

As the new government formed, Adams was wary. Never comfortable giving power to "strangers," he fretted over what was beyond the control of his community. Nor did it help his mood when in the elections to the First Congress, he lost to the arch-Federalist Fisher Ames. Elsewhere in the state, victory went to men with equally strong Federalist credentials. Some might rejoice that the new government was in the hands of its friends. Adams had a different view.

In 1789 the reconciliation between Adams and Hancock was made complete. With the governor's support, Adams ran for lieutenant governor and despite bitter opposition from the Federalists who suspected his commitment to the new government, he won handily. Not long after the election, Adams shared his thoughts with Richard Henry Lee:

> The Powers vested in Governments by the People, the only just Source of such Powers, ought to be critically defined and well understood; lest by a Misconstruction of ambiguous Expressions, and by interested Judges too, more Power might be assumed by the Government than the People ever intended they should possess. Few men are contented with less Power than they have a Right to exercise, the Ambition of the human Heart grasps at more. This is evinced by the Experience of all Ages.

Adams viewed the federal government as a political carnivore whose natural prey was state sovereignty. Should the beast go unbridled, "despotism" would surely result.

Together Adams and Hancock stood for reelection year after year, and with each new year the people of Massachusetts returned the two icons to office. They were unassailable. Sadly, Adams's triumph at the polls was proof of his growing irrelevance. Still preaching the Puritan covenant, government founded on virtue but wrapped in his romantic notion of a Christian Sparta, Samuel Adams was a quaint reminder of the past rather than a vibrant leader for the commonwealth's future. The people of Massachusetts elected him lieutenant governor largely because the post was ceremonial. Samuel Adams won his elections because his election did not matter.

Late in the morning of 8 October 1793, a messenger arrived at Adams's home. He brought bad, but not unexpected, news. Governor Hancock had died. Samuel Adams was the governor. His first task was to pay his respects to his friend.

It was a grand funeral. If Hancock had planned it himself, it could not have been more majestic. Solemnities began promptly at 3 P.M. The cortege left the Beacon Hill mansion and went straight across the Common to Boylston Street, where it took a left and paused at the site of the Liberty Tree. The procession then continued up Washington Street to the State House, around the building, and then to Old Granary Burial Ground, where the governor was laid to rest. When the cortege left Hancock's home, Samuel Adams was at its head, along with the governor's widow and family; a host of other dignitaries followed immediately behind. Adams walked with difficulty. It was clear to all that the new governor was not well. He was determined, however, to honor his friend. But age and illness took their toll, and he left the procession at State Street, just shy of its final destination.

Adams the Jacobin republican was an anomaly in Massachusetts politics. At a time when the state was firmly under Federalist control, he stood apart. Had they been fearful of Samuel Adams, the Federalists would never have permitted him to remain governor.

But both in Massachusetts and the nation at large the Federalists wielded such overwhelming influence that they could well afford to grant tolerance and respect to the ancient voice of Samuel Adams. He would remain in office until he voluntarily retired in 1796.

After paying homage to Hancock in his first inaugural address, Adams reiterated the principles that had governed his political life. He repeated his warning about the encroaching power of the federal government. "Should not unremitting caution be used, lest any degree of interference or infringement might take place, either on the rights of the Federal government on the one side, or those of the several States on the other?" He then went on to extol the "social compact" and "natural rights."

As long as Adams trudged through the realm of the abstract, his listeners nodded away. At one point in his speech, however, he lighted on a touchy subject, the French Revolution.

Having put their king and queen to death, established a republic, and then marched on their neighbors in the name of "liberty, equality, and fraternity," the French had lost the sympathies of conservative Federalists. Although no American could celebrate the more extreme aspects of the Revolution, Adams was clearly in support of republican France. Taking the occasion of his inauguration to praise the new republic Adams even went so far as to suggest that the constitutions of the two republics—America and France—agreed "in the most essential principles upon which legitimate governments are founded." Those principles were "liberty and equality." He went on to assert, "Indeed, I cannot but be of opinion that when these principles shall be rightly understood and universally established, the whole family and brotherhood of man will then nearly approach to, if not fully enjoy, that state of peace and prosperity which ancient philosophers and sages foretold."

Although increasingly enfeebled, Adams continued to stand for election annually, and the people continued to support him. On 4 July 1795 Adams, in company with Paul Revere, laid the cornerstone for the new statehouse designed by Charles Bulfinch. The cornerstone was drawn to the spot by 15 white horses, symbolic of the 15 states in the union. The entire legislature attended and saluted their venerable governor with a chorus of applause.

On 27 January 1796 Governor Adams addressed the legislature. A long and nostalgic speech began with the news, by this time known to nearly all, that President Washington had determined "to retire from the cares of public life." Adams heaped praise on Washington, who had "served with purity of intention and disinterested zeal." Not surprisingly, Adams made no mention of, nor extended good wishes to Washington's successor, John Adams. His cousin was a staunch Federalist whose politics were anathema to Samuel's republican instincts.

Perhaps it was in reflecting on Washington's departure from the stage and his cousin John's ascension to the presidency that Samuel took note of his own accumulating years. Toward the end of his message, he introduced a personal note. It was the patriarch's farewell. At 75 years old, he had "arrived to a stage of life marked in holy writ. The infirmities of age render me an unfit person in my own opinion, and very probably in the opinion of others, to continue in this station." As he moved away from the speaker's desk, this frail old man stumbled and nearly toppled to the floor. Even his worst enemies in the chamber were moved by the pitiful sight of his departure.

Nostalgia passed quickly, and within days the Federalists were ready to grab the seat so long denied them by Hancock and Adams. In the spring, Increase Sumner, the man Adams had defeated in the previous election, won the governorship. From his home, Adams could only watch in dismay as his Federalist foes whipped the public into a frenzy of anti-French hysteria, which culminated in 1798 with the passage of the Alien and Sedition Acts, a series of measures intended to bridle free speech and an open press. For Samuel Adams, who had helped lead a nation to independence through the power of the press, such measures were abominable.

When Virginia asked other states to join in protesting these measures, the Massachusetts legislature refused. The state attorney general then launched an action against Boston's *Independent Chronicle* for daring to criticize the legislature on that score. In an effort to silence the newspaper, the authorities jailed Abijah Adams, the paper's bookkeeper. Samuel Adams was so appalled despite his weakened condition, he asked to be taken to the jail so he might visit Abijah Adams and offer support.

In the men rising to power, Adams saw the same haughty, aristocratic disdain for virtue that he had once condemned in Hutchinson, Oliver, and the others. Power had corrupted the Federalists just as it had corrupted their ancestors. Confronted by evil and burdened by years, Adams did what his radical Puritan ancestor Roger Williams had done in similar circumstances: He withdrew from the world into the sanctity and purity of his own home. His withdrawal was not complete, however, for he did find one person for whom he felt closeness and admiration—his friend of 1776, Thomas Jefferson.

Adams and Jefferson shared a common ideology. They were republicans who had an abiding faith in the ultimate wisdom of the people and republican government. Jefferson, the sophisticated traveler, slave owner, and planter, was an odd match for "Sam the Publican," a man who never left his country and whose property and lifestyle were quite ordinary. Yet despite their worldly differences, they held a single faith.

After a gap of more than 20 years in their friendship, Adams wrote to Jefferson in January 1799. The sage of Monticello wasted no time responding. He told Adams how pleased he was that his old friend had written. Adams had expressed his concerns over the future of the Republic should it be left in the hands of the Federalists. Jefferson agreed. Both men decried the heavy national debt incurred by the Federalists. They were particularly concerned that so much of the treasury had gone toward creating an army, a machine that was always an enemy to republican government. One had only to witness what had recently transpired in France, for with Napoleon's overthrow of the republic, the threat seemed all the more immediate.

Jefferson's election in 1801 was a tonic to the aging Adams. He rejoiced when he read the new president's inaugural address, which pledged a return to republican and revolutionary principles. He shared with the new president the belief that the American republic was in fact "the world's best hope" for the preservation of liberty and freedom.

Adams never wavered in his faith in America. He understood that sin could draw people from the righteous and virtuous path, but he also believed in reform and redemption. In his last letter to none other than Thomas Paine, he took the old revolutionary to task. How could the author of *Common Sense* and *The Crisis*, essays that "awakened the public mind, and led the people loudly to call for a declaration of national independence," write the scurrilous *Age of Reason*, which extolled "infidelity"? Without religion, virtue was an orphan. Without virtue, the Republic could not survive.

By the fall of 1803 death was visible. Adams could barely walk, his mind had lost its edge. He told his family that when the time arrived, there should be no elaborate funeral. He wanted to leave the world in the same manner in which he had lived in it—simply. Early on Sunday morning, 3 October 1803, Samuel Adams died peacefully, with his family surrounding him. Within the hour, the bells of Boston sounded their lamentations.

Bibliography

❖
❖

It is not my intent here to provide a definitive, or even a lengthy list of sources. I have, for example, made no attempt to list journal sources. The following are works I have found useful and accessible.

Samuel Adams was always able to speak himself, and so in writing this biography I have tried as much as possible to return to his own words. The most extensive published collection of his writings remains Harry Alonzo Cushing (ed.), *The Writings of Samuel Adams*, 4 vols. (New York, 1904). However, given his long career and involvement with nearly every major revolutionary figure, the papers of many other people contain important Adams materials. Among those I have found most useful are W.C. Ford (ed.), *The Warren-Adams Letters*, 2 vols. (Boston, 1917–1925); L. Kinvin Wroth and Hiller Zobel (eds.), *The Legal Papers of John Adams*, 3 vols. (Cambridge, 1965); and Lyman Butterfield (ed.), *Diary and Autobiography of John Adams*, 4 vols. (Cambridge, 1961). Of course, letters mentioning Samuel Adams are often as informative as letters written by him. In this regard, for the years before the Revolution, Edward Channing and Archibald Cary Coolidge (eds.), *The Barrington-Bernard Correspondence* (Cambridge, 1912), is particularly useful. In addition, while Adams's newspaper contributions are in Cushing, it is necessary to examine the local papers to gain a sense of the context in which he was writing.

Since Adams played such a visible role in town and colony politics, both the *Journals of the House of Representatives of Massachusetts* (Boston, 1919–) are informative as are *The Journals of Each Provincial Congress of Massachusetts in 1774 and 1775 and of the Committee of Safety* (Boston, 1830). For town involvement, see William H. Whitmore et al. (eds.), *Boston Town Records*, 29 vols. (Boston, 1880–1902). Adams's career in the Continental Congress may be traced in W.C. Ford (ed.), *The Journals of the Continental Congress*, 34 vols. (Washington, 1904–1937) as well as the microfilm edition of the papers of the Continental Congress. Also important for his congressional years are Edmund C. Burnett (ed.), *Letters of Members of the Continental Congress*, 8 vols. (Washington, 1921–1936), and the more recent ongoing project of Paul H. Smith (ed.), *Letters of Delegates to Congress, 1774–1789*, 18 vols., in progress (Washington, 1976–).

Surprisingly, there have not been many biographies of Samuel Adams. The first comprehensive account was written by his great-grandson William V. Wells, *The Life and Public Services of Samuel Adams*, 3 vols. (Boston, 1865). Other major biographies since that time include James K. Hosmer, *Samuel Adams* (Boston, 1885), and John C. Miller, *Sam Adams: Pioneer in Propaganda* (1936). Pauline Maier provides a very insightful sketch in *The Old Revolutionaries* (New York, 1980).

Generations of historians have focused on the era of the Revolution. Adams is nearly always mentioned. Political theory for the period has best been analyzed by Bernard Bailyn, *The Ideological Origins of the American Revolution* (Cambridge, 1967), and Gordon Wood, *The Radicalism of the American Revolution* (New York, 1992), as well as his earlier *The Creation of the American Republic* (New York, 1969). Also useful are volumes 1 and 2 of Oscar and Lillian Handlin, *Liberty in America, 1600 to the Present* (New York, 1986–).

On the colony level much can be learned from the important work of Robert E. Brown, *Middle Class Democracy and the Revolution in Massachusetts, 1691–1780* (New York, 1955), as well as Stephen E. Patterson, *Political Parties in Revolutionary*

Massachusetts (Madison, 1973). Events surrounding the Massachusetts constitution are detailed in a lengthy introduction followed by documents in Oscar and Mary Handlin, *The Popular Sources of Political Authority* (Cambridge, 1966). G. B. Warden, *Boston 1689–1776* (Boston, 1970), describes the politics of the town as does Richard D. Brown, *Revolutionary Politics in Massachusetts: The Boston Committee of Correspondence and the Towns, 1772–1774* (Cambridge, 1970). Also useful in understanding the politics of Boston in the years before the Revolution is John Tyler, *Smugglers and Patriots* (Boston, 1986). For a congressional view of the revolutionary years, Edmund C. Burnett, *The Continental Congress* (New York, 1941), remains a classic. On the military side, the same may be said for Christopher Ward, *The War of the Revolution,* 2 vols. (New York, 1952).

Adams's colleagues have often been the subject of biographies. Among the best is Bernard Bailyn, *The Ordeal of Thomas Hutchinson* (Cambridge, 1974). See also William M. Fowler, Jr., *The Baron of Beacon Hill: A Biography of John Hancock,* and John Waters, *The Otis Family in Provincial and Revolutionary Massachusetts* (Chapel Hill, 1968). No one writing about early America, let alone Massachusetts, should miss John Langdon Sibley, *Biographical Sketches of Those Who Attended Harvard College,* 16 vols., in progress (Boston, 1873–).

Robert Gross (ed.), *In Debt to Shays* (Boston, 1993), examines the origins and impact of that rebellion. A broader view is provided by Van Beck Hall, *Politics Without Parties* (Pittsburgh, 1972). The struggle for ratification of the federal Constitution is described in Samuel B. Harding, *The Contest over the Ratification of the Federal Constitution in the State of Massachusetts* (New York, 1896).

On-line catalogs have made bibliographic work easier; however, they have not replaced the standard sources. In this regard three bibliographies remain immensely helpful: Ronald M. Gephart (comp.), *Revolutionary America, 1763–1789 A Bibliography,* 2 vols. (Washington, 1984); John D. Haskell (ed.), *Massachusetts: A Bibliography of Its History* (Boston, 1976); and Roger Parks (ed.), *New England Additions to the Six State Bibliographies* (Hanover, N.H., 1989).

Index

❖
❖

Adams, Abigail, 144
Adams, Abijah, 175
Adams, Elizabeth (Rolfe), 34, 37
Adams, Elizabeth (Wells), 1,
   140, 153, 160
Adams, Hannah, 1, 37, 49, 159
Adams, Henry, 2
Adams, John (grandfather of
   Samuel), 3
Adams, John 2, 19, 41, 45, 73, 90
   Massacre Trial, 107–112,
   130,132,133,138,139,144,151,
   153,157,162,165,175,
Adams, Joseph (son), 36
Adams, Joseph, (brother), 32
Adams, Mary,(sister), 32
Adams, Mary (dau), 37
Adams, Mehitable, 20
Adams, Samuel
  death, 1–2
  ancestry, 3–4
  childhood, 11–12
  Latin School, 12–14
  Harvard, 15–20, 24
  early career, 24–26
  early politics, 26–29

  marries Elizabeth Rolfe, 33
  opposes Albany Plan, 36
  defies sheriff, 37–38
  Writs of Assistance, 43–45
  admires James Otis, 46
  elected tax collector, 49
  writes instructions May 1764,
    52–53
  marries Elizabeth Wells, 54–55
  election to House, 62
  role with mob, 65–66
  Stamp Act, 62–71
  elected clerk of House, 72
  relations with Hancock, 73
  Townshend Acts, 74
  nonimportation, 75–77
  circular letter, 82–83
  troops in Boston, 85–99
  massacre, 102–104
  massacre trial, 105–112
  committee of correspondence,
    116–119
  Tea Act, 122–123
  Tea Party, 124
  elected to First Continental
    Congress, 130

Adams, Samuel (*continued*)
  Philadelphia, 131–132
  Lexington Green, 136–138
  Second Continental Congress,
    138
  election of Washington as
    Commander in Chief, 139
  Bunker Hill, 140
  independence, 144
  role in Congress, 146–155
  controversy with Hancock,
    155–156
  Massachusetts Constitution,
    156–159
  elected to state senate, 162
  Shays's Rebellion, 164–167
  federal constitution, 167–172
  elected lieutenant governor, 172
  governor, 173
  death, 177
Adams, Samuel (father),
    10–11
  land bank, 21–24, 32
Adams, Samuel (son), 36,
    140–141,153, 170
Age of Reason, 177
Aix la Chapelle, Treaty of, 32
Albany, 148
Albany, Congress, 35
Albany, Plan, 36
Alien and Sedition Acts, 175
Allegheny River, 35
Allen, James, 32–33.
Ames, Fisher, 172
Andover, 19
Andros, Edmund, 87
Annapolis Meeting, 167
Anti-Federalist, 169
Appalachian Mountains, 49
Arbella, 5
Articles of Confederation, 153,
    162
"Association," 134

Baltimore, MD., 147–148
Barbadoes, 11
Barnard, John, 18–19
Barnstable, 40, 119
Barre, Isaac, 59–60
Barrons, Benjamin, 43–44
Beacon Hill, Boston, 73, 81
Beaver, 122–123
Belcher, Jonathan,18, 22
Berkenhout, John, 154
Bernard, Francis, 40, 44, 61, 64,
    67, 68, 80, 84, 85, 86, 92, 100
Bethune, George, 18
Bill of Rights, 171
Billerica, 138
Bishop in America, 46, 75
Bordeaux, 153
Boston, xi, xii
  founding and early history, 5
  development of town meet-
    ing, 6–9
  Latin School, 11–14
  economic distress in 1740s,
    20–21, 30–32
  Stamp Act riots, 64–67
  troops, 83–84
  massacre, 103–112
  Tea Party, 122–124
  evacuation, 143, 146
  ratification convention meets
    in, 168–172
Boston Common, 91, 109, 136
Boston Neck, 64
Boston Port Bill, 125
Boston Society for Encouraging
    Trade and Commerce, 44
Bowdoin, James, 130, 157, 164,
    165, 167, 169
Brainerd, David, 27, 29, 47
Braintree, Mass., 3, 73
Brandywine, Penn.,150, 152,
Brattle Street Church, 89
Bristol (England), 3

Bristol County, Mass., 23
Brookline, Mass., 124
British Coffee House, 97
Brutus, 62
Bulfinch, Charles, 174
Bunker Hill, 140–141
Burgoyne, John, 148, 150–151
Burke, Edmund, 53
Bute, John Stuart, Third Earl, 64
Butler, Samuel, 71

Caesar, Julius, 62
Cambridge, 14, 108, 124,
    134–135, 136, 140
Camden, Lord, 78
Canada, 39, 148
"Candidus", 90, 116
Carolinas, 146
Carpenters's Hall, 132
Carthage, 125n
Castle William, 43, 64, 107, 110,
    126, 128
Cato, Marcus Porcius, 125n
Caucus, 10n
Charles I, 62
Charles II, 87
Charles River, 127
Charleston, S.C., 31, 111, 159
Charlestown, Mass., 123
"Chatterer", 108, 109
Checkley, Samuel, 33, 55
Checkley, Hannah, 3
Checkley, Elizabeth, 33–34, 37, 159
Chesapeake Bay 148
Circular Letter, 79, 82, 83–84
Clap, Thomas, 28
Clarke, Jonas, 136
Clarke, Richard, 122
Cockle, James, 44
Coercive Acts, 125–127
Coffin, Nathaniel, 67
Colman, John, 21, 24

Customs Commissioners, 75, 79,
    91
Committee of Correspondence,
    116, 119, 121, 123, 124
Common Sense, 177
Concord, Mass., 134
Concord River, 138
Connecticut, 127
Continental Congress, First,
    128–144 Second, 138, 142,
    145–160
Convention of Towns, 87–88
Conway, Thomas, 152
Cooke, Elisha, 10
Cooke, Elisha, Jr., 10, 24
Cooper, Samuel, 89, 94, 105
Cooper, William, 89, 92
Copley, John Singleton, 55, 103
Cornhill, 102
Cornwallis, Charles, 159–160
Covenant, Adams's and Puritan
    conception, ix, xi, xii, 6, 16,
    19, 27, 77, 114
  Mass. Constitution (1780),
    157–159
The Crisis, 177,
Cromwell, Oliver, 62
Curwen, Samuel, 138
Cushing, Thomas, "Death's
    Head," 24–25
Cushing, Thomas, 51, 73, 130,
    131, 132, 138, 142, 164, 165

Dalrymple, William, 105, 107–108
Dartmouth, 122–123
Dawes, William, 137
Deane, Silas, 127, 154
DeBerdt, Dennys, 78
Declaration of Independence,
    102, 119, 144
Declaratory Act, 71, 74
Declaration of Rights, 134

Dedham, Mass., 146
Delaware, 148
"Determinatus," 83
Dinwiddie, Robert, 35
Dock Square, Boston, 103
Dominion of New England, 87
Dorchester, Mass., 124
Downe, Samuel, 18
Duche, Jacob, 132–133

East India Company, 122
Edes, Benjamin, 64
Edwards, Jonathan, 30
Eleanor, 122–123
Ellery, William, 147–148
Essex Street, Boston, 68
Eustis, William, 151
Exchange Tavern, Boston, 21

Fabian tactics, 147
Faneuil Hall, 65, 123, 129
Faneuil and Winslow, 123
"A Farce," 165
Federal Constitution, 167
    ratification in Massachusetts,
        167–172
Federalists, 169–170, 174, 175
Fifield, Mary, 4
Fifield, Richard, 4
First Church, Boston, 103
Fishkill, N.Y., 148, 151
Fort Ticonderoga, N.Y., 148, 149
Fourteenth Regiment, 110
Fowle, Daniel, 26
Franklin, Benjamin, xi, 35, 58,
        121, 144, 154
France, 148, 152–154
French and Indian War, 35–36

Gage, Thomas, 67, 128–130,
        134–136

Gardiner, Sylvanus, 163
Gates, Horatio, 149, 150, 152,
        159
Galloway, Joseph, 132, 133
George II, 43
George III, 43, 134
Georgia, 95
Gerard, Conrad, 154
Germantown, Penn., 150, 152
Gerry, Elbridge, 117, 142, 146,
        168
Geyer, George, 97
Glorious Revolution, 16
Great Awakening, 28
Green Dragon Tavern, Boston,
        170
Greene, Nathanael, 159–160
Greenleaf, Stephen, 37, 67
Grenville, George, 50, 54, 64,
        70–71, 126
Greyhound Tavern, 84
Griffin's Wharf, 124
Guy Fawkes Day, 17n, 63

Hagar (slave), 34
Hague, The 162
Hallowell, Robert, 146
Hampshire County, Mass., 78
Hancock, Dorothy Quincy, 55
Hancock, John, xi, 1, 19, 47, 55,
        73, 80–82, 96–97, 105,
        115–116, 118, 129, 134–135,
        139, 142, 145, 149–150, 152,
        155, 160, 161, 163, 164, 165,
        167–172, 173
Hancock, John George Washing-
        ton, 170
Hannibal, 147n
Hanover County, Va., 62
Harrington, James, 16
Harvard College, 14, 15–25 108,
        140
Harvard Hall, 16

Harvard Yard, 15
Hatfield, Mass., 163
Haverhill, Mass., 34
Hawley, Joseph, 142
Henry V, 114
Henry, Patrick, 62
Hillsborough, Lord, 82
Holyoke, Edward, 19
Holyoke, William, 20
Howe, William, 148, 150
Hudson River, 148
Hutchinson, Anne, 41
Hutchinson, Elisha, 122
Hutchinson, Thomas, 22, 35, 36,
    38, 39, 41–42, 44–45, 64, 66,
    68, 79, 85, 86, ,90, 95, *
    100–101, 103–112, 113, 115,
    118, 119–120, 121, 122,
    124–125, 128–129, 166

Independedut Advertiser, 26
Independedut Chronicle, 175

Jackson, Richard, 66, 86
James II, 3
Jay, John, 132, 155
Jefferson, Thomas, ix, xi, 102,
    119, 133, 144, 176
Journal of the Times, 90–92
Judges's salaries, 79, 117

Kemble, Margaret, 128
Killroy, Matthew, 110
King George's War, 32–33
King Street, Boston, 102, 129
Kilby Street, Boston, 64

Land Bank, 20–25, 30
Lee, Arthur, 113, 116, 124, 154
Lee, Henry, 22

Lee, Richard Henry, 144, 168,
    172
Leeds, Duke of, 149
Lexington and Concord battle,
    136–138
Liberty, sloop, 80–82
"Liberty Bowl," 82
Liberty Tree, 68, 69–70, 84, 123
Lillie, Theophilus, 99
Lincoln, Benjamin, 166
Livingston, Robert R., 144
Locke, John, 16
Long Wharf, Boston, 31, 75, 128
Lovell, John, 12
"Loyal Nine," 63–64

MacIntosh, Ebenezer, 63–65, 67,
    69–70
Madeira wine, 80
Madison, James, ix
Marblehead, Mass., 119
Marshall, Captain, 80
Massacre Day oration, 114, 135
Mass. Board of War, 156
Mass. *Centinel,* 164
Mass. Charter (1629), 8,–9
Mass. Constitution (1778),151,
    153, 156
Mass. Constitution (1780),
    157–159
Mass. Court of Vice Admiralty,
    66
Mass. Hall (Harvard), 16
Mass. Provincial Congress,
    134–136, 141, 145–146, 156
Mass. Senate, 162
Mather, Cotton, 4, 48
Mather, Maria, 4
Mather, Increase, 4
Mauduit, Jasper, 58
Mein, John, 96–97
Mobs, 63, 85,
"Mohawks," 124

Molineaux, Will, 107, 125
Monogahela River, 35
Montgomery, Hugh, 110
Montreal, 39
Morris, Robert, 162
Mulliken, Lydia, 137

Napoleon, 176
New Hampshire, 95
New Jersey, 110, 128, 146, 148
New York, 31, 54, 93, 97, 111,
    122, 127, 142, 145, 152, 153
Newbury Street, Boston, 64
Newman, Robert, 137
Newport, R.I., 97, 153
Nonimportation, 76, 93–95, 111
Norfolk, Va., 31
North, Frederick, Lord, 122,
    125–127
North Bridge, Concord, 138
North Church, Boston, 137
North End, Boston, 63, 136
Northampton, Mass., 28, 142

"Observer," 164, 165
Old South Church, Boston, 11,
    123–124, 135, 146
Oliver, Andrew, 41–42, 60, 64,
    68, 70, 83, 109, 113, 121
Oliver, Peter, 72
Otis, James, Senior, 40
Otis, James, Jr., 19, 41–42, 44–46,
    51, 58, 61, 68, 73, 81, 85,
    97–98, 119, 164
Otis, Joseph, 119
Otis, Ruth Cunningham, 55

Paine, Robert Treat, 129–130
Paine, Thomas, 177
Palmer, Mass., 153
Paris, Treaty of (1763), 48

Paris, Treaty of (1783), 163
Parker, John, 137
Partridge, Oliver, 61
Paxton, Charles, 66
Pennsylvania, 142, 146
Penn, William, 27
Pennsylvania *Chronicle*, 92
Pennsylvania State House, 132
Petersham, Mass., 166
Philadelphia, Penn., 31, 54, 92,
    93, 97, 111, 122, 127, 130,
    131, 138, 145–146, 147, 148,
    149, 152,
Pitcairn, John, 136
Pitt, William, 39, 58, 78
Plymouth, Mass., 119
Pollard, Colonel, 38
Pope's Day, see Guy Fawkes Day
Pownall, Thomas, 39–40, 41, 43
Prescott, Samuel, 137
Preston, Thomas, 103
Princeton, N.J., 148–149
Proclamation Line 1763, 49
Puritanism, influence on early
    Boston, 4–6

Quebec, 39
Queen Street, Boston, 102
Quincy, Josiah, 107–112, 119

"rateable estate," 10
Reed, Joseph, 132
Revere, Paul, 82, 104, 114, 127,
    136–137, 170, 174
Richardson, Ebenezer, 99
*Rights of the British Colonies As-
    serted and Proved*, 52
Rippon, HMS, 100
Robinson, John, 97–98
Rockingham, Charles Watson-
    Wentworth, 2nd Marquess,
    71, 78

Rogers, Gamaliel, 26
Rolfe, Elizabeth (first wife of Samuel), 34
Rolfe, Elizabeth, (mother of Elizabeth), 33–34
Rolfe, Mehitable, 34
Rome, 76, 125n, 168,
Rowe, John, 73, 111
Roxbury, Mass., 84, 124
Ruggles, Timothy, 61, 69
Rush, Benjamin, 147

Saint Paul, 161
Salem, Mass., 44, 125, 129, 134, 138
Sanford, Margaret, 41
"Sans Souci," 164–165
Saratoga, N.Y., 150, 152
Savage, Samuel Phillips, 155
Schuyler, Philip, 149
Scottish Society for the Propagation of Christian Knowledge, 28
Sewall, Jonathan, 44
Sewall, Stephen, 40
Shawmut, 6
Shays's Rebellion, 165–167
Shelburne, William Petty Fitzmaurice, Earl of, 78
Sherman, Roger, 144
Shirley, William, 35, 36, 38, 41
Smith, Francis, 136
Snider, Christopher, 99, 114
Solemn League and Covenant, 127
Sons of Liberty, 68, 69, 71, 84, 76, 122, 131
South Carolina, 133
South End, Boston, 63
South End Gang, 69
Springfield, Mass., 166
Stamp Act, 54, 56, 58, 60–71, 73
Stamp Act Congress, 61, 68–69

Stamp Act Repeal, 70–71
Story, William, 66
Stoughton Hall, 16
Sudbury, Mass., 7, 48, 120
Suffolk County, Mass., 130
Suffolk Resolves, 133
Sugar Act, 50–54, 57–58, 63, 70

Taxes, external versus internal, 59
Tea Assembly, 164–165
Tea Part, see Boston Tea Party
Temple, John, 154
Tennant, Gilbert, 28
Thacher, Oxenbridge, 51, 61–62, 68
Throat Distemper (diptheria), 20
"A Tory," 108
Townshend Duties, 74, 77
Townshend, Charles, 59, 74, 126
Trenton, N.J., 148–149
Twenty Ninth Regiment, 103, 107, 110
Tyler, Royall, 51

"Valerius Poplicola," 117
Vermont, 166"Vindex," 88, 90, 108, 110, 116
Virginia 133, 127, 146
Virginia Resolves, 62
Virginia House of Burgesses, 62

Wadsworth, Benjamin, 15, 18
Wadsworth House, 15
Ward, Artemus, 163
Warren, James, 119, 143, 160, 161, 164
Warren, Joseph, 19, 55, 81, 130, 133, 135, 140, 141, 151
Warren, Mercy Otis, 164, 165

Washington, George, 35, 139, 145, 146, 147, 149, 150, 152, 174–175
Webb, Hannah, 3
Wells, Elizabeth, 55
Wells, Francis, 55
Wells, Thomas, 1, 159
West Indies, 11, 51
Whately, Thomas, 54, 121
Wheelwright, Nathaniel, 57, 61
Wheelwright's Wharf, 107
White, Hugh, 102
Whitefield, George, 28
Whittelsey, Chauncey, 28
Wilkes, John, 80
William, 122

William and Mary, 3, 87
Williams, Nathaniel, 11
Williams, Roger, 176
Winthrop, Governor John, 3, 5
Winthrop, John, 169
Woburn,Mass., 138
Worcester, Mass., 78
Worcester County, Mass., 138
Writs of Assistance, 43

Yale College, 28
York, Penn., 150
Yorktown, Va., 162
Young, Thomas, 94, 114, 116–118

NATIONAL UNIVERSITY
LIBRARY   SAN DIEGO